BEV JAMES is a successful entrepre business performance expert, coach speaker with over twenty years' experience transforming businesses in diverse sectors including coaching, training, recruitment, sales and health and fitness.

As the founder and managing director of the Entrepreneurs' Business Academy she has joined forces with James Caan, one of the stars of BBC TV's *Dragons' Den*, to provide a unique training and mentoring programme for ambitious entrepreneurs. Together they have created a 'success blueprint' that can positively transform the productivity and profitability of any business.

Bev is also MD of The Coaching Academy, the world's largest training organisation for coaches, and a multimillion-pound business. She runs both organisations from her offices in Richmond, Surrey.

A Master NLP (neuro-linguistic programming) Practitioner and a European Master Trainer for DISC personality profiling, Bev has vast experience of recruiting high-performing teams, of talent management and high staff retention, particularly in challenging environments. She has coached many entrepreneurs to the success they enjoy today and is widely regarded as a millionaire mentor. She has a thorough understanding of the mindset and skill set characteristic of entrepreneurs and business owners. Bev is a regular columnist in the entrepreneurial and business press with wide media experience.

www.bevjames.com

DISC is a personality profiling technique that originated from the work of Dr William Marsden. Throughout my business career DISC has proved to be one of the most powerful assessment tools I have ever come across. It is simple to use and easy to understand. I use the principles in every aspect of my life to assist with decision-making, team building and negotiation. It is explained in full in Chapter 3.

"The must-read book for every entrepreneur at all stages of business building, particularly *before* big ideas are launched."
James Caan, Founder and CEO of Hamilton Bradshaw

"Bev is one of life's exceptional people [and] a great testament to the adage 'anything you want can be achieved - the only thing that will stop you is yourself.' I think the book title says it all and is Bev all over. I am sure the book will inspire many to take positive action."
Jamie Constable, Founder and CEO RCapital

"*Do It! or Ditch It* is an exciting, accessible introduction to a set of the most useful decision-making tools for entrepreneurs and business owners. It is comprehensive, highly readable and filled with useful examples."
Darren Shirlaw, Founder of Shirlaws Coaching and Navitas IP

"*Do It! or Ditch It* - definitely a book for those serious about achievement. Clear, direct and inspiring. Just do it and reap the rewards."
Richard Denny, Author of *Selling to Win*

"Bev James shows you not only the route to your success - but explains the step-by-step actions to get you there."
Peter Thomson is regarded as one of the UK's leading strategists on business and personal growth

"*Do It! or Ditch It* is an excellent reminder of what really matters in the process of creating a successful business. Genuine passion, learning and giving are essential components... The power of this book lies in the fact that Bev is a living example of what she is teaching."
Tony Banks, Chairman of Balhousie Care Group and self-made millionaire, featured in *The Secret Millionaire* (Channel 4).

"*Do It! or Ditch It* is an insightful coaching book for business owners and potential business owners, and is a highly useful tool."
Gill Fielding, Entrepreneur and and self-made millionaire, featured in The Secret Millionaire *(Channel 4).*

"Grounded, practical, inspiring and warm, Bev James offers valuable advice and tools which will help any wannabe entrepreneur to make the dream a reality."
Simon Middleton, founder of Brand Strategy Guru and author of *Build A Brand In 30 Days*

"Bev James has been there and done it, from initial dream through to final implementation... [she] can show you how you can have your own success as well."
Mark Rhodes, Motivational Speaker, Business Mentor and Entrepreneur

"As a business expert and turnaround specialist for a new generation of millionaires, Bev understands how business leaders think and why they behave the way they do..."
Emma Wimhurst, Author of *BOOM!*

"*Do it! or Ditch It* is an immensely informative book for people pre start-up and throughout their business journey."
Amanda Morreale, Publisher/Editor *The Market*

"Bev has created a gem of a book with *Do It! Or Ditch It*. Her passion shines through on every page, as does her determination to succeed … This is definitely the book for those people who are ready to take action and take their business to the next level."
Karen Moxom, Managing Director of the Association for NLP and Publisher, Rapport

"…Bev is an authority on the application of DISC and its use in business, sales, and interpersonal relationships and we have been honored to support her expertise. …"
Brad Myers (CEO, PeopleKeys) and Deanna Miller (Operations Manager, PeopleKeys

"The best thing in life is achieving what people said you could not do! Not just another business book, a truly useful guide that is both developmental and practical."
Sally Poinsette, CEO, Anouska Hempel Design

"Sometimes a book comes along that you you pick up and can't put down because of the great business sense it offers. Bev James has written such a book… the boost you know you most need, right NOW!"
Ann Skidmore, Award-Winning Image & Leadership Coach

"I have witnessed Bev's pragmatic, insightful and inspiring business coaching, style and quality first hand, for many years. She has now skillfully crystallized all of that into *Do It! or Ditch It*."
Greg Brown, Managing Director and Executive Coach, GB Executive Solutions Ltd

"When an influential businesswoman such as Bev James commits her expert knowledge to paper, the rest of us need to take note of every word. From title to final sentence this book is crammed full of useful and inspiring material, all delivered in her passionate but practical and no-nonsense way."
Tim O'Rahilly, Business Coach & Education Consultant

"A must-read for anyone looking for success in life! … in [Bev's] unique, 'shoot from the hip' style."
Andy Smith, Founder and Managing Director, Electric Wholesale Ltd

"…*Do It! or Ditch It* is a fabulous coach in book form, to get people started on the right foot and not the back foot, to create success that lasts."
Thomas Power, co founder of www.ecademy.com

"A successful lady, who has helped many successful people, Bev's book will help you to choose where to focus your time and when to let go.… Knowing when to 'do it or ditch it' is a critical skill to learn. Bev has put her heart into this book, combined with her commercial mind – a winning combination."
Penny Power is co founder of www.ecademy.com and author of *Know Me, Like Me, Follow Me*

"… If you are serious about being the best, take heed of Bev's advice and you too could have success you've so far only dreamt of."
Pam Lidford, Personal Performance Trainer and Coach

"Thoughtful, clear and insightful business gems …"
Oliver McNeil, Legend Photography

"… *Do It! or Ditch It* will make things happen for everyone who reads it."
Charles Lucas FCA, Accountant and financial advisor to Bev James, and Chairman of Broadthunder Limited

"This is a must read for any aspiring entrepreneur. By following Bev and her team's effective techniques our company exceeded £1 million turnover in our first full year of operation. Bev has now put the wealth of her experience on paper. I therefore highly recommend this book."
Alyas Khan, CEO, EMICA

"…the perfect essential read for the budding entrepreneur or business person."
Toby Garbett, World Champion & Olympian, Personal Trainer

"… accessible and informative. Bev's energy for getting things done is infectious …"
Nikki Wild, Managing Director, Wild Empowerment Ltd

"A delight to read. Informative, motivational and thought provoking … packed with useful tips proven to springboard you to achieving your goals.
David Wilson, Dentist, Coach and Mentor to those living with persistent pain

If you want to turn your ideas in to action and ensure more business success, *Do It! or Ditch It* moves you forward with inspiration. … highly recommended – let it inspire you to take your business success to highest level.
Maria Deacon-Viney, Chartered FCIPD, Remarkable Success Coaching and Consulting

"This book should come with a prescription and a warning: Apply the advice and techniques liberally and it will change the performance of your business, your attitude and your life."
Sue Blake, EBA PR Expert, Profile & Publicity Development & Management Specialist

DO IT!
OR
DITCH IT™

Turn ideas into action
and make decisions that count

**EIGHT STEPS TO BUSINESS SUCCESS
FROM THE MILLIONAIRES' MENTOR**

Bev James

Bev James

Virgin BOOKS

11

First published in 2011 by Virgin Books, an imprint of Ebury Publishing
A Random House Group Company

Copyright © Bev James 2011

www.randomhouse.co.uk

Address for companies within The Random House Group Limited can be found at
www.randomhouse.co.uk/offices.htm

The Random House Group Limited Reg. No. 954009

A CIP catalogue record for this book is available from the British Library

ISBN: 978-0-753-53999-6

Penguin Random House is committed to a sustainable future for
our business, our readers and our planet. This book is made from
Forest Stewardship Council® certified paper.

Printed and bound in Great Britain by Clays Ltd, St Ives plc

Design: carrdesignstudio.com

To buy books by your favourite authors and register for offers visit
www.randomhouse.co.uk

Printed and bound in Great Britain by Clays Ltd, St Ives plc

DO IT! or DITCH IT is dedicated to
the memory of Pete Regan

CONTENTS

Acknowledgements

I am a firm believer in the pure power of goal setting and this book sees the fruition of one of my major life goals now achieved. I now know the process of birthing a book intimately. It has been the most extraordinary year of my adult life and one I am most grateful to have experienced. There are many people I would like to thank for their support and especially for the support, love and care shown to me during the past year, when writing and running businesses has been intense, challenging, exciting and always full-on.

My special thanks to my husband and soul mate, Dave, for your love and unconditional support, for sharing my belief that anything IS possible and for being my rock. My love and thanks to my Mum and Dad who continually support and believe in me. You've empowered me from such a young age to set goals. My sister and best friend, Dee, for always being there for me. My gorgeous niece, Kelly and her boyfriend, Amish. Guys, I wish I'd had your confidence and business acumen when I was your age. The world IS your oyster. Continue to grab it with both hands as I know you will. My nephew Dean, a skilled builder, who makes me laugh with his quick wit and quirky sense of humour, which has been much appreciated during the past year when I have been burning the candle at both ends with my projects. My special thanks and appreciation to my No.1 fan, Uncle Gord.

My sincerest thanks to each member of my incredible team who make the impossible possible on a daily basis. You never fail to impress me. You are amazing individuals and collectively an awesome team.

My thanks to the dedicated team of trainers and course managers at The Coaching Academy. You are truly amazing examples of coaches at the top of their game, inspiring others with your passion, expertise and commitment to the coaching profession.

I'd like to express my appreciation to the Entrepreneurs' Business Academy team of Millionaire Mentors and Experts. You are the finest examples of what it takes to be successful in business. I feel honoured to know and work with you all.

My grateful thanks to James Caan for writing the Foreword and to the team at Hamilton Bradshaw, all of whom embrace the 'can do' attitude.

Jamie Constable and Peter Thomson, my mentors, you have inspired and influenced my business life beyond belief and for that I am truly grateful to you.

Good times with my family and friends are what makes my life worthwhile and I am blessed to be surrounded by people who I love and admire and to work with committed, talented and passionate people in all areas of my professional life.

And last but by no means least, sincerest thanks to my editor, Ed Faulkner, and the team at Virgin Books; my agent, Sheila Crowley, for seeing the vision; Sue Blake and Sarah Sutton for helping me organize my thoughts, keeping me on track and for making this book a reality.

FOREWORD

Vibrant and thriving entrepreneurialism lies at the heart of the recovery of the UK economy. I'm always frustrated to read the latest start-up enterprise failure statistics when they are released annually. Each stat represents not just the loss of a business or venture but the loss of a livelihood, hopes and dreams. During this recession there have been major job cuts across the board. I know many people who have used redundancy as an opportunity to start a new life by becoming their own boss and I applaud their courage and determination. I've long held the belief that it isn't what happens to us in life that matters, but what we do in response to our experiences. Success requires a combination of positive attitude, drive and unquestioning belief in what you are doing. As business owners, we also need to have a clear sense of self: our strengths, weaknesses and beliefs.

I've known Bev James since November 2009, when we created the Entrepreneurs' Business Academy. Bev is a superb co-founder and Managing Director. She brings a wealth of business knowledge to our joint venture, coupled with her immense business coaching expertise and people management skills. We launched the business in a recession and everything we advise our business delegates to do, to grow their businesses, we are doing with our own. The success of the EBA isn't down to luck or reputation only.

When Bev told me she was writing *Do It! or Ditch It* I was really pleased. I know so many people who have a passion for their first big idea for a business, but too many of their subsequent business decisions are based on emotional assumptions rather than commercial reality. With a staggering number of starts ups not reaching year two, *Do It! or Ditch It* is the perfect tool to help focus plans and clarify decision-making before setting off. A start-up entrepreneur will find Bev's book invaluable; as will an established business owner who wants to launch a new brand or create a new venture.

I encourage you to view Bev as your personal business coach. Her approach, through *Do It! or Ditch It*, uses years of business experience to guide you through your business journey. Like me, she knows a great business will only deliver to its full potential with the right leadership, attitude and team in place. If you apply the *Do It! or Ditch It* methodology to your business decisions, you'll increase your chances of success in all areas of your life exponentially.

James Caan, June 2011

Preface

'We are judged in life not by our intentions, but by our actions. Life is too short to allow our energy to dwindle by being busy with things that are going nowhere.'

- Do you struggle with managing your time and your workload?
- Do you wish you could get more done in a day?
- Do you find you are 'managing upwards' because someone else has trouble making decisions?
- Are you in a position where you need to influence others' decisions?
- Do you want to 'ditch' procrastination and 'do' the things that will propel you forward with success?

Welcome to the world of *Do It! or Ditch It* thinking – where decision-making is clear and everything is possible. It all depends on how far you want to go with your dreams and plans. Effective decision-making lies at the heart of progress in every area of life – but never more so than in the workplace. The ability to make fast and effective decisions and to be able to communicate effectively is vital for everybody involved in business; whether managing their own workload or someone else's. It's not just the business owner who influences outcomes. It is those around them, too. Everyone has personal responsibility for their own actions. *Do It! or Ditch It* will help you to develop the discipline to make focused decisions, use your time wisely and get to where you want to be.

WHO IS THIS BOOK FOR?

Much of *Do It! or Ditch It* is aimed at business owners and entrepreneurs, because more people than ever before are likely to aspire to set up their own venture; but it is for those who are 'intrepreneurs', too: employees who want to make a good idea great; who can see new ways to do business or simply want to be more effective at decision-making within a corporate environment. Many more people are taking control of their own financial destiny by becoming one of a new breed of 5–9ers who are earning an additional income. Anyone with a goal needs to focus on making consistently effective decisions in order to know when to act – and to know when to walk away. Do It! or Ditch It thinking will help you to succeed.

Television has turned entrepreneurs into household names and media stars. Multimillionaires are now famous in their own right and are becoming modern-day role models. Young people in particular want a slice of the lifestyle that their success represents. A challenging job market is prompting more 17–25-year-olds to take the plunge and dive into running their own venture, even though the waters are unknown and can be murky. However, the average age of owner-managers or sole traders remains 40-plus. Some, when faced with redundancy, have taken the opportunity to set up on their own, rather than trying to search for a new job. There is no such thing as a job for life any more. The availability of training schemes and the potential to reach the marketplace via new technology means that starting up in business has never been easier or more attractive. All you really need is a computer, a mobile phone, a business idea and the market know-how to get started. Many people begin by choosing to create a web-based business.

Generally speaking, successful entrepreneurs are go-getters who understand that making an informed decision or taking a calculated risk – even if in retrospect it is a 'wrong' decision – is better than making no decision at all. Decisions lead to action. Learning from mistakes helps us to become more resilient and wise. Decision-making propels us forward; it brings about change, and it makes things happen. Staying in business for the long term, by creating a successful enterprise that keeps on growing, depends on the decisions that you make each day.

Statistics show that more people from every section of society are taking the plunge and making the decision to set up in business.

UK Small Business Statistics:

- There are 4.8 million small businesses in the UK.
- 3.6 million businesses are sole proprietors.
- 97 per cent of firms employ less than 20 people.
- 95 per cent employ less than 5 people.
- Over 500,000 people start up their own business every year.
- Less than 9 per cent are under 35, although this sector is increasing in numbers.
- Small and medium-sized firms employ more than 59.8 per cent of the private sector workforce.
- Small firms contribute more than 49 per cent of the UK's turnover.
- 64 per cent of commercial innovations come from small firms. micro: 0–9 employees, small: 10–50 employees, medium: 50–249 employees.

(Federation of Small Businesses, updated October 2010)

USA Small Business Statistics:

The estimated 29.6 million small businesses in the United States:

- Employ just over half of the country's private sector workforce.
- Include 52 per cent home-based businesses and 2 per cent franchises.
- Represent 97.3 per cent of all the exporters of goods.
- Represent 99.7 per cent of all employer firms.
- Generate a majority of the innovations that come from US companies.

(Source: US Small Business Administration Office of Advocacy, September 2009)

- There were 627,200 new businesses, 595,600 business closures and 43,546 bankruptcies in 2008.
- 7 out of 10 new employer firms survive at least two years, and about half survive five years. Findings do not differ greatly across industry sectors.

(Source: US Small Business Administration Office of Advocacy, September 2009)

Women in Business
UK

- Nationally, about 30 per cent of self-employed women work from home.
- Whereas 60 per cent of self-employed women in the North East had incomes of £10,000 or less in 2006/7, a little under half those in London, the South East and East of England earned this amount. Similarly, the proportion of self-employed women who earned less than £5,035 in the North East was 4 percentage points higher than the proportion across the UK as a whole (11 and 7 per cent respectively).
- 82 per cent of self-employed women work alone or with a partner.
- Nationally, 29 per cent of self-employed people are women.

(Women in Business, ONS, 2009)

There is much discussion about gender differences in business. I believe that the main difference lies in the initial motivation to start up a business. Many women begin working from home to give them flexibility around childcare. Statistically they are more likely to ask for business advice early on – which suggests that their early confidence may be lower than men's; and statistically, also, there are more male than female business owners. However, in the big scheme of things, there is no difference at all. Every business person, whatever their age or gender, needs to be equally commercial in approach to get results.

US

- The number of women-owned firms continues to grow at twice the rate of all US firms (23 vs. 9 per cent). There are an estimated 10 million women-owned, privately held US businesses. The greatest challenge for women-owned firms is access to capital, credit and equity. Women start businesses for both lifestyle and financial reasons. Many run businesses from home to keep overhead low.

(Source: SBA, Office of Advocacy and Business Times, April 2005)

- Women represent more than 1/3 of all people involved in entrepreneurial activity.

(Source: Global Entrepreneurship Monitor (GEM) 2005 Report on Women and Entrepreneurship)

- Women are more likely to seek business advice – 69 per cent women vs. 47 per cent men.

(Source: American Express)

Minority-Owned Business

- Black-owned businesses are the fastest growing segment, up 45 per cent between 1997 and 2002. Revenues generated by the nation's 1.2 million black-owned businesses rose 25 per cent between 1997 and 2002 to $88.8 billion in 2002.

(Source: US Census Bureau)

Seniors in Business

- Entrepreneurship among seniors is growing. In 2002, the rate of self-employment for the workforce was 10.2 per cent (13.8 million workers), but the rate for workers aged 50 was 16.4 per cent (5.6 million workers). Although those aged 50 made up 25 per cent of the workforce, they comprised 40 per cent of the self-employed. Solo business formation in the future will be driven by people who take early retirement or whose jobs just disappear.

(Source: AARP/Rand Corp. 'Self-employment and the 50 Population')

US statistics reproduced from SCORE www.score.org http://www.score.org/ small_biz_stats.html Retrieved 26 March 2011

Interesting Facts about Young Entrepreneurs

'The last six years have seen a 46% jump in the number of graduates describing themselves as self-employed or freelance. It has risen from 4,190 in 2002–03 or 2.9% of employed graduates leaving university – to 6,130, or 4.1%, in 2008–09.'

Lucy Tobin in the *Guardian*, 30 November 2010

Mark Zuckerberg was just 20 and still a student at Harvard University when he and some friends launched Facebook in February 2004. He remains the majority share owner. The company is estimated to be worth around $50 billion.

Alex Tew from Wiltshire in the UK, launched milliondollarhomepage.com in 2005 as a quirky route to raising funds to cover the cost of his Three-year business management degree. The home page consists of 1 million pixels in a grid. Pixels were sold for $1 each, in blocks of 10x10, to be hosted for five years. The final 1,000 pixels were auctioned on eBay. The whole project generated income of £1,037,100 and spawned a whole new way of Internet trading.

Ashley Qualls makes over $70,000 per month from her website whateverlife.com. She started up with an $8 domain name in 2004. In 2006 she negotiated a deal with ValueClick Media, an online media brokering firm. The owner had no idea she was only 14.

Steve Bennett founded Software Warehouse in his 20's after being made redundant. He became a serial entrepreneur and now runs The Colourful Co. Group Ltd with his brother, John, which includes the online auction, Gems TV.

Alexander Levin founded ImageShack in 2003 when he was only 18. Now 26, his estimated net worth is $23 million.

Sam Walton, founder of Wal-Mart, delivered newspapers, milked cows and sold magazines for money while attending high school.

Sir Richard Branson, billionaire owner of the Virgin group of companies, started out selling vinyl records from his car in his late teens.

Dominic McVey created his UK-based business, importing scooters, at the age of 13. By the age of 15 he was a millionaire. He says, 'I didn't set up in business to make money, I set up to prove teenagers can achieve success. Kids are always being told "You can't do this, you can't do that."' Now 29, he runs a portfolio of businesses.

'Stop talking about it ... get on with it. Because if you don't, in a year's time you will see someone else doing it.'

Dominic McVey

During my career I have built several significant businesses during periods of recession, including the Entrepreneurs' Business Academy with investment dragon James Caan. As a business coach and mentor, I have worked with a broad range of businesses and with many millionaires. I have an absolute passion for people and business. My mission is to deliver to as many people as possible the skills and coaching insights that I have used to build my businesses and have shared with my clients, and I hope that as a reader you will feel supported and encouraged along your business or career path.

Do It! or Ditch It was born of the frustration of seeing too many good business ideas go to waste while bad ideas take up valuable time and resources – and from a strong desire to show that we are always in control of our own decisions and can choose to make things happen if we wish. The approach can be applied to all situations.

My profession is all about helping people to make decisions that create the outcomes they really want in life. I spend a lot of time listening to people describe their next great idea, or coaching them as they talk about their future intentions. I get great satisfaction from playing a part in those ideas coming to fruition. But I have also met other, would-be entrepreneurs, in more social situations, who get stuck along the way. We all know people who have good ideas that never seem to take off. Month after month the idea is talked about, but it always remains a tantalising glimmer on the horizon. Nothing ever happens. The passion and drive are slowly clouded by talk of 'should', might', 'could'.

Brian Tracy, in his book *No Excuses*, refers to a place he calls 'Someday Isle', meaning *someday I'll* … He says that many people go off to an imaginary place called Someday Isle; a place where they are going to live their best life *someday*. They say things like, *someday I'll* set up my own business, *someday I'll* travel; *someday I'll* learn a new skill. If you ask them when they are going to do it, you will find that they have perfected a story about why they can't have what they want and often include the word *but* in their sentence: I'd like to *but*; someday I will *but*; I would if I could *but* … If we feel we have created enough excuses we can feel OK about not taking action. It is the difference between dreamers and dream makers: one thinks about doing it, the other gets on and does it.

> **'Where are you going with your business idea? Are you are you already planning a successful journey? Or are you headed for "Someday Isle"?'**

It is as a result of having one too many of these kinds of conversations with a friend that I resorted in frustration to saying: 'I have been hearing you talk about this for years but you've done nothing about it. It's time to just bite the bullet and either Do It! or Ditch It, for good.' It's a direct approach that I sometimes use as a business coach or mentor, too. In this case it worked; and both my friend's business and the idea for my book were born.

That was also when I realised that there were many other people out there who were facing the same kind of inertia and lack of confidence. The seed of the idea of the Entrepreneurs' Business Academy was also planted at that moment.

MY STORY: FROM DELEGATE TO MD IN 1,000 DAYS

As founders of the Entrepreneurs' Business Academy (EBA), James Caan and I aim to provide a unique training and mentoring service for ambitious entrepreneurs to help transform their productivity and profitability. I am also MD of The Coaching Academy (TCA), the world's largest coach training organisation and a multimillion-pound business. My business journey owes a great deal to the Do It! or Ditch It techniques.

In 2005, on the recommendation of a friend, I attended one of their courses. I went along mostly out of curiosity. I certainly had no burning desire to train as a coach and was already a specialist in DISC personality profiling and a Master Practitioner of NLP. Once there, however, I was so impressed by the trainers' passion for coaching that I was hooked. My trainers that weekend were Sarah Urquhart, Ann Skidmore and Pam Lidford. They were clearly at the top of their game; they were incredibly knowledgeable and very generous with their time, willing to share their vast experience with the audience. In addition, they were approachable, warm and extremely humorous! I was impressed that they each made a full-time living as a coach and had all trained with TCA. By lunchtime I knew that I had found something very special.

Having been inspired by the experience, I now wanted to be not only a fantastic coach but I also wanted to be a trainer for TCA, and to join their world-class team. I remember returning to the training room before the afternoon session on the second day and standing at the front of the room imagining that *I* was a trainer for the Academy. Deep in thought, and imagining myself in the role, I stood by the projector and looked around the room as if it were full of delegates and I was taking the session. I was soon jolted back to reality when a fellow delegate asked me what on earth I was doing. I said, 'I am going to be a trainer for The Coaching Academy and I am going to be standing right here.' She laughed and suggested that I had better sit down before the real trainer came in. However, within six months I had completed my training, set up a successful coaching business, with paying clients.

I was still hungry to learn more, and I was so impressed by what I had experienced that I offered to help out for free at future weekend events. I was running my own business, so this was a significant time commitment, but I wanted to gain insights into how the events were run. I watched the trainers and learned from them; I spoke to delegates and got to know what they wanted from a training provider. I set up the room, got the trainers their tea and coffee, and did my best to make sure the event ran like clockwork. This time was invaluable – I didn't get paid at first but I learned an enormous amount.

One Sunday, after helping out at the morning session, I had an opportunity to speak to the MD of TCA. My coaching business, called Elements Coaching, was growing well and I was utilising DISC profiling as part of my coaching practice with all of my clients. As a Master Practitioner for DISC personality profiling in Europe, I considered it an essential coaching tool and suggested that TCA should offer a DISC training day to coaches. I explained how I had set up my coaching business and the marketing methods I had used to generate more clients than I was able to cope with. The last session of the two-day coaching course was about how to get clients. Seeing my obvious passion for coaching and marketing know-how, the MD asked if I would like to become a trainer for TCA and deliver the last session of the weekend.

At that time, I had a self-limiting belief about standing in front of 100-plus people, which was the size the group was likely to be. I was comfortable working with groups of thirty but this was definitely taking me out of my comfort zone. With my heart in my mouth and my kneecaps jumping I said a very confident 'yes' to the opportunity, and tried to ignore the butterflies in my stomach. I called my session 'Turning your Passion into your Profession' and found that I really enjoyed delivering it to a room of appreciative delegates. I was so full of the excitement of my own coaching journey that I could sense some of that buzz was being projected onto the delegates in my sessions. This turned out well for TCA as many delegates were inspired by my coaching journey and felt the same buzz that I had experienced. I would like to think that it was one of the reasons that TCA enjoyed one of its best years for new recruits.

Not everything we do needs to have a price attached to it. Sometimes the greater value lies in the knowledge learned and the experience gained. As a TCA trainer I wanted to know as much as I could about the courses on offer. I chose to attend every TCA diploma course in my own time so that I could tell new delegates about the course content from first-hand experience. If I was going to promote TCA, even on a voluntary basis at first, I wanted to know about every course and every trainer. I felt privileged to be learning from the best in the business. I also offered to make 'follow-up' calls after every training weekend so that I could find out why some people chose not to continue on to the diploma courses. I offered to do this for free because I wanted to know if it was related to the cost of training, or a lack of belief in the viability of setting up a coaching business. My assumption was that if delegates had a fantastic experience at the introductory weekend, they were more likely to decide to take a diploma course – which would benefit them, their future clients, as well as TCA as a business. I became more and more involved in TCA, and during my time as a trainer I delivered part of the Small Business Diploma, as well as courses on NLP, DISC and the certificate weekend courses. I loved what I was doing.

There is a saying in life that you should be careful what you wish for because it might just happen. TCA changed hands in November 2008 and, *exactly 1,000 days* after I had attended my first training day I walked through the doors as the newly appointed managing director. It was a very exciting day for me.

The first twelve months were difficult, to say the least, because I took over TCA as a worldwide recession began. It was difficult because the coaching industry had not been through a recession previously, which meant that there were no records, statistics or indications of how a recession would affect this type of business. The early part of the first twelve months was challenging as revenue was unpredictable. It seemed the general public was uncertain about the future, and many people became indecisive and unsure about what to do. Happily, by the end of the first twelve months, we had increased net profit by 25 per cent; annual staff sickness was reduced from thirty days in the previous year to zero and the revenue per staff member increased by £100,000. The lesson was that many people choose to up-skill during a recession and some seize the opportunity to set up their own business.

The secrets of our success? I had to take some very hard decisions early on – and one of those was to reduce staff numbers. Following reorganisation, I had to ensure the team were positioned to play to their core strengths, which I did using DISC profiling. Two years later my team is running TCA and helping me grow the Entrepreneurs' Business Academy (EBA), too. It has been a steep learning curve, and I have loved every minute of it. The Do It! or Ditch It approach coaxed me out of my comfort zone and into my 'stretch zone' of personal growth and possibility. Through the EBA and TCA the approach is being shared with hundreds of new delegates every month, too.

Key decision-making stages

- Having a clear vision.
- Being willing to step out of a personal comfort zone for a worthwhile goal.
- Directed focus and determination.
- Building strong relationships.
- Seeing an opportunity and acting upon it.
- Knowing how to hire, train and work with the best people.
- Being prepared to do whatever it takes, no matter what.

It was mainly due to single-minded focus and a passion for the work that I succeeded. I didn't set out to become MD of TCA; I set out to learn as much as I could about the training, and I loved the process so much that I wanted to encourage as many people as possible to sign up for courses. That in itself propelled me forward. I was also extremely aware of my own self-limiting beliefs and I didn't want anything to get in the way of succeeding. As a result I was hungry to learn. I invested in courses that helped me to overcome my fear of public speaking and so on. I dedicated all my spare time to learning about coaching and how to be an effective coach. Ultimately I was in the right place at the right time, with the right experience. My story proves that anything is possible – it depends on the choices you make and how you choose to use your time.

'Anything is possible – it depends on the choices you make and how you choose to use your time.'

INTRODUCING THE
'DO IT! OR DITCH IT' APPROACH

*'In your moments of decision
your destiny is shaped.'*

Anthony Robbins

Being successful begins with a positive mindset and with positive behaviour that supports your goal. Each of us makes thousands of decisions and hundreds of choices during the hours we are at work each day. Cumulatively they have a profound impact on levels of success and the direction that life takes. Who we know, where we live, where we work, what we have achieved, who we live with: everything is the result of decisions that we have made in our lives so far. Every thought you have contributes to your actions, and every action is a decision that takes you closer to or further away from your goal.

To quote Stephen Covey, you need to 'Start with the end in mind'. Each of the techniques in *Do It! or Ditch It* is designed to encourage you to ask each day, 'What behaviour will set me on course to achieve my goal?' Success in some form will eventually come if we keep those behaviours going in a focused direction.

The 'Do It! or Ditch It' approach is clear, focused and practical – and is based on my own experiences as a business mentor, leadership coach and a business owner. Part I includes five decision-making tools that you can apply in a fast, focused and considered way. Part II will show you how to apply each of these steps to different areas of your business.

FIVE TOOLS FOR FOCUSED DECISION-MAKING

Do It! or Ditch It includes a decision-making dashboard that will enable you to beat procrastination, decide on your core priorities and make appropriate decisions.

THE DO IT! OR DITCH IT DECISION-MAKING DASHBOARD

1. **Enter The Stretch Zone** See page 22
2. **Focus Your Mind: On A Scale Of 1 To 10** See page 41
3. **DISCover who you are** See page 56
4. **Review The Swot Spot** See page 77
5. **Look Back From The Future** See page 86

Each of these tools will help you to decide what to DO! and what to DITCH.

EIGHT STEPS TO TAKING ACTION

Do It! or Ditch It will get great ideas on track, and help you to ditch the ones that have missed their moment, lost their momentum or just aren't going to work. Each of the eight steps improves the quality of daily decision-making and increases clarity, transforming good ideas into commercial reality, making every choice a conscious decision and turning plans into positive action.

Step 1	**What?**	What's the big idea?	**Evaluation**
Step 2	**Why?**	Why is your idea important to you?	**Motivation**
Step 3	**Where?**	Where are you heading?	**Planning**
Step 4	**Who?**	Who do you need to help you deliver?	**People**
Step 5	**How?**	How will you achieve your goal?	**Sales and Marketing**
Step 6	**How much?**	How much will it cost? Is it profitable?	**Finance**

| Step 7 | **When?** | When will you see results? | **Management** |
| Step 8 | **Do It!**
or Ditch It | Making a decision | **Taking stock** |

Every step includes personal success stories and Do It! or Ditch It decision-making tools to keep you focused on whether your project is on track, whether plans need adjustment, or whether your decisions are taking you nowhere, fast.

My wish is to help good ideas maintain their momentum – and to prevent terminal drift. The eight-step process is designed to fire up enthusiasm and sharpen focus. Deciding it is time to 'do or ditch' your favourite idea will set you free to focus on something new – or spur you into making it happen. Remember – your decisions shape your destiny.

HOW TO USE THIS BOOK

Do It! or Ditch It is divided into two parts. Part I describes the five foundation stones of decision-making. Part II applies those tools to eight different business areas. Underpinning the whole book are the principles of DISC – a powerful technique that will help you understand why and how you make decisions.

Some people will want to start at the beginning; others will dip into the chapters that seem most useful. Wherever you start, the book is designed to help you to challenge your thinking and make each decision count.

'It's not *where* you begin – but *why* you begin that matters.'

DISCover YOUR DECISION-MAKING STYLE

*'Businesses don't fail – people do. Sadly,
usually the only thing that has got in the
way of success is themselves.'*

The Do It! or Ditch It approach combines motivational thinking with practical action and includes a simple approach to personality profiling called DISC (see page 44). You will learn whether you are Dominant, Influencing, Steady or Compliant and how your core character influences the way you make decisions. Once you understand your DISC profile and how your style impacts on other people, you can use DISC to raise your skill levels whenever required, and to consider decisions from others' viewpoints.

During my work with many successful business people, multimillionaires and world-class sportsmen and women, I have seen time and again that the characteristic that sets many of them apart is their ability to make focused and effective decisions that take them single-mindedly towards their dream and their goal.

Some people are born with the drive to succeed; others develop it more slowly. But everyone has the ability to get to the top – provided they want success badly enough. Businesses don't fail – people do. Sadly, usually the only thing that has got in the way of success is themselves. I want to help every entrepreneur to make effective decisions that will help them to deliver both their short-term priorities and long-term strategic plans. Making good decisions depends on having a clear idea of where you are headed and what you want to achieve – and then having the self-discipline to see your plans through. As the adage goes: 'People don't plan to fail, they fail to plan.'

'People don't plan to fail, they fail to plan.'

Whether you are thinking of starting up in business or are already running a company, the Do It! or Ditch It approach to planning, testing and evaluating will get you out of your comfort zone and help you to become more effective and more profitable in everything you do. It will encourage you to look back from the future – to make all of today's decisions count towards achieving your vision of tomorrow, such as expanding the scope of your current business. The path is not for everyone. It requires toughness, self-discipline and single-mindedness – but it is ultimately extremely rewarding. I know the approach works – it worked for me and it works now for my business clients.

THE GOOD, THE BAD AND THE UGLY OF BEING IN BUSINESS

The challenges, the uncertainty and the responsibility of going it alone do not suit everybody's nature, no matter how commercially savvy they may be. It is better to recognise from the outset where the boundaries of your comfort zone lie, rather than setting sail on a commercial path towards a destination you would rather not reach. I call it the good, the bad and the ugly of being in business.

The good

1. You are the master of your own destiny. You can choose the direction of the company.
2. You can choose who you work with.
3. You can decide when and where you work.
4. The sense of personal satisfaction when you succeed will be immense.
5. There is no limit to the level of income you can potentially earn; and there is the chance of becoming financially independent if you are able to sell the business for a healthy sum.

The bad

1. You are likely to find yourself working long hours, possibly without holidays.
2. You will have to recruit, manage and discipline staff.
3. There could be sleepless nights when things don't go to plan.
4. You may know when things aren't right but not know what to do about it.
5. You may know what to do but not have the resources to do it.
6. You will have to take tough or uncomfortable decisions.

The ugly

1. If things go wrong there is no one else to blame.
2. If things go wrong there can be a lot to lose.
3. Personal financial guarantees can come back to haunt you if the business fails.
4. Personal confidence can take a major knock if things don't work out.
5. A poor financial track record can limit future borrowing opportunities.
6. You may have to get a job and go back to working for someone else.

The greatest fear of many employed people is losing their job. The greatest fear of most entrepreneurs is that they may have to get a job! *Do It! or Ditch It* focuses on everyday traits of business behaviour: bringing out the proactive and the positive in every business owner, to help them to make conscious decisions that increase everyone's chances of commercial success.

> *'The greatest fear of many employed people is losing their job. The greatest fear of most entrepreneurs is that they may have to get a job!'*

PART I

HOW TO DEVELOP
A 'DO IT!' MINDSET

Five decision-making tools

Chapter 1

MAKING DECISIONS FOR LIFE

'Every life is lived forwards, but can only be clearly understood by looking backwards.'

- If you are employed and facing redundancy, would you choose to focus on job hunting? Or would you focus solely on setting up your own business?
- If you have to prepare for an important business meeting, but a close friend pleads with you to attend a social occasion, do you drop everything and go? Or do you remain firmly focused on your goal?
- If you are at your computer, mid-task, deep in concentration, perhaps short of time, and an email arrives. Do you answer it immediately?
- If your in-tray has reached overflow, how do you prioritise? Do you start with the task that will deliver the most money? Do you focus on the one that will create trouble if neglected? Or do you focus on the detail and start organising into categories?

I learned very early on that we are judged in life not by our intentions, but by our actions – and that life is too short to allow our energy to dwindle by being busy with things that are going nowhere. Life is for living – and for achieving – and we owe it to ourselves to become the best we can be. Sometimes that means knowing when to 'ditch' the things that aren't working for us, as well as having the courage of our convictions to 'do' the things we are passionate about, and the self-discipline to stay focused on those things that will take us in the longer term to where we want to be.

DEFINING MOMENTS

People often ask what drives my business decisions and my ambition to succeed and where it started. On a simple level I can say that my passion for business has always been rooted in the desire to do something that I love and to do it well. At a deeper level, and with the benefit of hindsight, I can see the defining moments in my life where I have been so committed to a course of action that the outcome has radically shifted the direction of my business future. The key question at the heart of all these situations was: 'How can I make things happen?'

Everyone has moments in life that impact on their confidence to make important decisions. It can be helpful to reflect on those moments, to understand more about what drives you and what helps or hinders your own decision-making.

Defining moment No. 1: Living life 'as if'

Our attitudes and choices are usually rooted in an experience of childhood. In my case, it was the desire to own something so badly and so madly that my single-minded determination drove me to earn as much money as I could. Like many children, I wanted to own a horse. I knew that horses weren't cheap! I had a lot of money to save. But as a result I began to get invaluable early business training – without realising it.

My dad was good with money and never went into debt for anything, but we certainly weren't wealthy. Thankfully, both my parents were employed and held the same jobs for more than forty years and, like many people of their generation, they worked hard and set the standard for us to have a strong work ethic in our family. My sister and I had to earn our pocket money by doing cleaning chores and, if we wanted anything our pocket money couldn't buy, we had to earn it by working.

I have fond memories of working at the local lido when I was about 11 years old. The lido was an open-air swimming pool, boating lake and sunbathing area that was situated behind our house. A friend of my dad's was the manager there and he trusted my sister and me to help out. (The laws about minors working weren't as strict in those days.) My sister was older than me, so she worked in the snack kiosk and doubled up as a lifeguard, while I earned 50p a day by running the mini-golf course. The highlight for me at the end of the day was clearing up the rubbish around the grounds with a fabulous gadget that looked like a spear!

Sadly, after a while the lido closed down and my source of income disappeared – until someone bought the land and set up a boatyard in its place. The land was beside a lake, and as I walked down to take a look I noticed that all the boats were dirty. I had the first of my defining 'Do It!' moments when I asked, 'Can I clean the boats for you?' I could – and they paid me 50p per boat. I felt rich – and the possibility of getting my horse felt that much closer. I kept saving and believing that my dream would come true and looked for even more ways to increase my earning potential. There was a garden centre next to the boatyard and so I took the opportunity to help out there, too.

Before I had anywhere near the amount of money needed to buy a horse I truly entered the state of acting 'as if' I owned one. I used my savings to buy everything I would need for when I eventually got my horse. One by one, I bought the best grooming brushes, hoof oil, hoof pick – everything. I soon owned an impressive grooming kit and had even purchased a second-hand bridle. I used to sit in the living room taking it apart and cleaning it regularly. In fact, I would walk along the path near our house with my bridle proudly over my shoulder, so that I looked the part and everyone would think that I had a horse. I always faced the traffic, of course, so that everyone could see me … Most of my family thought I was mad.

In my spare time I used to visit a family friend called Dorcas, who let me ride her donkey, Mercury. Dorcas had recognised my passion and helped me to realise my dream. When I turned 12, she paid for me to have a block of riding lessons in an excellent riding school and brought me a complete riding outfit as a birthday gift. After the lessons ran out I continued to pay for more out of my pocket money.

At the age of 15, after years of saving, and with enormous help from my parents, I became the proud owner of my first horse, for which I am eternally grateful. I had agreed to earn enough money to pay for half the keep – and on the bright side, I didn't have to buy anything else because I had already purchased a whole shed full of tack and brushes. My dad got permission to keep the horse on the old lido site behind our house. Together, we eventually built a wonderful stable and yard. I mixed the concrete as my dad laid the bricks.

> *'If you believe strongly enough in your idea, and are committed to it, those around you are more likely to buy into it and believe in it too.'*

Defining moment No. 2: Start where you are

Wherever there are animals, there will be kids – and I discovered the local kids were always hanging around and asking to 'have a go' on my horse, named Fleck. Having an expensive hobby like owning a horse tends to change your approach to earning money ,and I was always looking for new ideas. In order to pay for Fleck's keep, I asked local parents if I could teach their children to ride, for half the price of a local riding school. I had been well taught myself, so it was all done properly. I insisted they wore safety hats and ran it as professionally as I could. The parents were happy because the field was visible from their homes, and the children were happy because they were having fun. In retrospect, this was my first experience as a coach. I loved it.

Looking back, I now also realise that I was developing commercial awareness. I was soon buying another horse – one that had been badly mistreated. He cost me £60 at the time, and six months later he was looking beautifully healthy, so I sold him to one of the girls I was teaching for £150 and also added the cost of livery on the field. It was a lot more than I would have earned doing the usual Saturday job or a paper round.

The lesson for me was, just start. Don't worry about 'if onlys'. Use what you have and build on that, rather than delaying your decisions because you would rather build a castle in the clouds.

The lesson for me was, just start. Don't worry about 'if onlys'. Use what you have and build on that.

Defining moment No. 3: Have the courage of your convictions

One of the things that influences decision-making is a willingness to have the courage of your convictions and to do things your way. When I left school at 16, I took a job at a local chemical factory for a while. The hours were short and the money was good, but it was solely a means to an end.

I knew that I wanted a different life and decided that I would train to become a gym instructor. I began studying books on physiology during my lunch breaks and a fellow worker who was a part-time physical training instructor helped me learn to pronounce some of the muscle groups and tested me to make sure I knew them all. It was a lot of work, but I qualified several months later. This now gave me the opportunity to earn extra cash, and I took an evening and weekend job in a local gym.

I had a real passion for gym instruction and soon realised that I would prefer to pursue this as a full-time career if the opportunity arose. I didn't have to wait long because, as fate would have it, a brand new gym was opening close to home and they were advertising for staff. I was given a job.

> *'It can be hard to choose to "go against the flow" because others may doubt your path and question your decision; friends can be lost. But it is important to remember that only you can know what you aspire to achieve. The decisions you make today will create the future you live tomorrow.'*

Defining moment No. 4: Keep pushing your personal boundaries

Every business owner has an opportunity to teach and lead their team, and at my new employers I was lucky to work for someone who saw my hunger to learn and respected my potential for progression. The fitness world fascinated me. I wanted to learn all I could about running the business, training the trainers and taking the exercise classes. It really was a case of learning through doing. I never held back from offering to take on more responsibility.

As the business expanded, so did my experience. Over time I became the business manager and when the business expanded and an opportunity arose to help set up new premises, I installed all the operational systems and procedures. Fortunately it wasn't a matter of choosing to forfeit my social life for my ambition as it was a very sociable environment. I enjoyed it so much, it didn't seem like work!

The business experience I got from setting up a new club from scratch was excellent. I was selling the concept to potential new members from a Portakabin within the building site. We put inspiring pictures on all the walls and arrows pointing inside to encourage people to come on in and sign up for membership.

Every sale solves a problem, and so I focused on why people wanted to join the club rather than getting bogged down in the detail of the floor plans. This was all about selling aspirations. Our members were buying the results they wanted to achieve, not the treadmill or bench press machines. By the time we opened the doors we already had more than 1,000 members.

I found that selling came naturally to me, and I enjoyed being in friendly competition with my team-mates. On the other hand, teaching aerobics took me well out of my comfort zone and I was nervous beyond belief before each class started, even though I was in my element as soon as it began. Feeling scared or nervous isn't a reason not to do something; it can be a sign of how important it is to you and, over time, I came to learn that the more you practise something the easier it gets (provided you are practising the correct things!).

> *'Fear is a warning sign that you are in an area of discomfort – but in the context of business, it isn't necessarily a sign that you shouldn't "have a go". We never know what we are capable of until we try. We can't gain experience from things we haven't done.'*

Defining moment No. 5: Confidence develops by learning through doing

People have said to me that I am lucky to be naturally confident, but that isn't necessarily the case. Determined – yes, always confident – no. I have spent most of my life in my 'stretch' zone and feeling terrified at times. I have learned that confidence develops by becoming comfortable feeling uncomfortable, and after a while you realise that you can deal with anything that comes your way. Regardless of the outcome, you *will* deal with it.

The desire to achieve my goals has always driven me through the fear factor, and my attitude has always been 'get over it and get on with it'. Worrying without acting never helped anyone.

During my years in the health club industry I gained experience through setting up beauty and hairdressing salons, running a small chain of owner-operator health clubs, and eventually leading the training and marketing strategies at national level for a PLC group.

> *'Always say yes to taking on more responsibility; or volunteer to help out, if there is an opportunity to learn and develop new skills. Confidence grows with depth and breadth of experience. Courage is being the only one who knows that you're afraid.'*

Defining moment No. 6: Taking a risk on DISC

A chance introduction to Dr William Marston's DISC personality profiling system was another defining moment in my life that stood out with absolute clarity from the outset. I could see the benefits of this amazing tool immediately. It was a methodology that changed the old-style mindset of 'treat others the way *you* want to be treated' to a new and far more effective approach of 'treat others the way *they* want to be treated'. I did a lot of research into DISC and ran DISC profiles on everyone I knew, which was great practice and reinforced my belief in the product.

During my research I discovered a company in Pittsburgh, Pennsylvania, USA, that had an excellent DISC product range. I was totally committed to making a DISC-orientated business work and so ordered £1,000 worth of their products to test the material. The products impressed everyone: the people I tested them on, as well as my now ever-growing customer base.

The company was called PeopleKeys. I rang to ask whether they had anyone representing DISC and their products in the UK and to suggest I should fly to Pittsburgh to meet them face to face – at my own expense. Within ten minutes of putting the phone down I had my flight and hotel booked. While testing the DISC materials, I had formulated an exciting idea that could turn out to be an additional product for them and another business opportunity for me.

I had used the DISC profiling technique to help identify the primary motivational triggers of each individual fitness club member. By applying the technique we could keep people motivated and engaged as long-term members. I invested in a marketing brochure to add the 'wow' factor. My gamble (that is, my calculated risk) paid off. The team at PeopleKeys liked the idea and I was invited to meet their owner/president, Dr Sanford Kulkin. Dr Kulkin liked my product too, and commented that, this was the first time that someone had ever taken the time to come all the way to Pittsburgh with something *for them* as opposed to wanting to take something away.

I returned to the UK as their UK Master Trainer and agent for the UK and Europe, with the go-ahead to develop my product further – with their support. I was excited, to say the least. This was a great opportunity and I couldn't wait to get started. And so I set up my first training company, called Elements Consulting.

**'Don't put a price tag on everything you do.
Invest in relationships and play a part in
other people's success.'**

Defining moment No. 7: People buy things to solve problems

Filled with enthusiasm and knowing that DISC was a fantastic product to sell, I wanted to build up the numbers as quickly as possible. Through a contact, I was introduced to the operations director of one of the world's largest high-street recruitment agencies. She wanted some help in making better in-house hiring decisions, to try to replicate the skill set of their top sales performers and ideally to improve team retention – all of which the DISC system could help provide.

I knew from our telephone conversations that she was a direct and detail-orientated individual, which meant that she would be testing the system (and me) rigorously. I was also aware that I would be competing with two larger companies that were already well established; however, I had confidence in my product knowledge and the value of the DISC method and, when the time came, it worked.

I was absolutely correct about her testing the system – and me! A fake profile was entered into the trial batch to see if the system could be manipulated. I spotted it, and in addition identified someone on her team who was on the verge of burnout. As the only one aware of the circumstances surrounding this individual, she was impressed that the DISC system could identify the situation. The contract was won and I secured an initial order of £65,000 that later turned into a worldwide contract.

> *'Always focus more upon what your prospective client needs, than on what you want to gain.'*

Defining moment No. 8: Where you start out is one thing; where you end up is your choice

In order to attract more corporate clients, we rented a mailing list and ran a direct mail campaign to promote a DISC training workshop. The first event had only two confirmed bookings, which was disappointing to say the least. Of course, you can't run a course with only two people – especially when it is your first one. My options were to:

- Cancel it.
- Rebook for a future date.
- Run it – but make it credible by adding a further six to eight people.

Many in that situation would probably think, 'That's not enough people – how can I get out of this?' I remember my own reaction: 'That's not enough people – how can I make this work?' Cancelling or rescheduling the event were not options. I had already booked rooms in which to run the workshop and my two prospective clients were flying in from Europe with flights and hotel accommodation already confirmed. Had we rescheduled, the chances were that my two clients would not have come back; they might have told other people about their experience and there would have been no opportunity to develop repeat business. I saw cancellation as potentially losing us thousands of pounds and it didn't feel like the right thing to do. There was only one option – run the course and make up the numbers from somewhere, to make it credible.

I decided to invite six friends and family along for the two-day workshop, including my niece, Kelly. All of them had business interests, which was encouraging, and Kelly was under strict instructions not to call me Auntie Bev for the whole two days! It was a high-risk strategy, and one that I wouldn't care to repeat – but it worked, and I made sure that every single one of the attendees benefited enormously from the event.

As we went round the room on the first day, the two genuine clients introduced themselves. They both worked for the same company, which was a luxury jewellery brand. One of them was the European HR director. When I asked for feedback at the end of the two days, he had one thing to say: 'I like this product. How do I buy?' Eight years later, they are still important clients.

The lessons learned from that episode were extremely valuable. I discovered that we needed a longer lead time if we were to fill the room, which would allow time to re-mail the prospect database. I also learned to respect my gut instincts and discovered that my reaction when things go wrong is to take action.

The training companies I now run drive in excess of 8,000 people to our various events and seminars each year. With an average of 100 people per course, it's a far cry from the two I had on my first course – but we all have to start somewhere. No matter what kind of business you are running, the key issues are exactly the same: does the business model stack up? And, if it does, how can I get more heads through the door, or more bums on seats, or (in the case of a hotel) heads on pillows.

The lessons I learned from these defining moments still stand me in good stead years later. They gave me the required experience to embrace the next steps of my business journey, but, most of all, I learned that committing to *doing* rather than bailing by *ditching* was the only way to kick-start a business.

'We can't gain experience from things we haven't done.'

GET COMFORTABLE FEELING UNCOMFORTABLE

It may sound like a strange thing to say, but in business you need to be comfortable feeling uncomfortable. If running your own business was easy more people would do it. The reason most entrepreneurs get excited about business is because it is a personal challenge and the results *aren't* guaranteed. We can win *or* lose. Sportspeople would soon lose interest in competing if they were guaranteed to win every event and so would most entrepreneurs. Most would agree that the harder the game, the greater the victory. I'm not suggesting we all want business to be a tough slog every day, but many entrepreneurs are at their best when they have to fight their way out of a corner. I describe it as being comfortable feeling uncomfortable. The more challenges you face in business, and the further you venture into your 'stretch' zone, the more likely you are to stay the distance and achieve the goals you seek (see page 22).

> *'If running your own business was easy more people would do it. The reason most entrepreneurs get excited about business is because it is a personal challenge and the results* aren't *guaranteed.'*

DO IT! OR DITCH IT

DECISION-MAKING TECHNIQUE

ENTER THE STRETCH ZONE

'A ship in harbour is safe – but that is not what ships are for.'

John A. Shedd

The difference between the entrepreneur who makes a success of his or her business and one who doesn't often comes down to sheer dogged determination and personal grit. It is not just your business skills that count under pressure – it is your character: your willingness to step outside your comfort zone, to try doing things in a new way, to take calculated risks and do what it takes to see you through.

HOW FAR CAN YOU STRETCH YOUR COMFORT ZONE?

Your future success frequently lies outside your comfort zone – in your stretch zone. That's where it's at. Simple. Those who are the most successful in business are constantly pushing their boundaries. They are the trailblazers and pioneers who welcome new challenges.

Successful businesspeople often say they welcome the feeling of discomfort that comes from knowing that something 'isn't quite right'. It is an entrepreneurial intuition that makes you stop and question what is happening and what you should do differently. It has the power to save the day.

Imagine three circles in one (as illustrated overleaf):

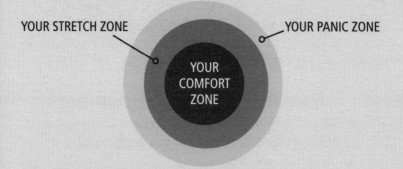

● **The inner circle is your comfort zone.** Imagine it to be green.
● **The middle circle is your stretch zone.** Imagine it to be amber.
● **The outer circle is your panic zone.** Imagine it to be red.

- The comfort zone is the least challenging. It is the circle of familiarity and habit. It is also the zone of the dreamer and Brian Tracy's 'Someday Isle' (see page xxv).
- The stretch zone is productive and energising for some and scary for others. This is the circle of learning and personal growth. This is the entrepreneur's zone of action.
- The panic zone is unpredictable. For most people it is debilitating and full of fear.

The important thing to know is where you are, which zone you find most motivating, which the most rewarding or empowering, and where you are most productive.

The panic zone is where you may end up if you do not plan ahead and anticipate problems. The panic zone will paralyse most people, though some may find it energising in short bursts.

Spending too much time in the panic zone may cause some people to retreat into their comfort zone for an extended period, having learned little and suffered much. Others will find the adrenalin-fuelled situation has stretched their boundaries, gaining them knowledge and experience.

However, it is unwise to spend too much time in the panic zone, as it will gradually erode your energy, and those around you may not be able to cope, as you may have to employ fire-fighting techniques at the last minute in stressful situations.

> **'It is unwise to spend too much time in the panic zone, as it will gradually erode your energy, and those around you may not be able to cope.'**

If you remain in your comfort zone for a long time, on a familiar and unchanging path, your comfort zone will actually shrink and your panic zone will increase in size, because the world around you will change and become uncomfortable:

YOUR STRETCH ZONE   YOUR PANIC ZONE

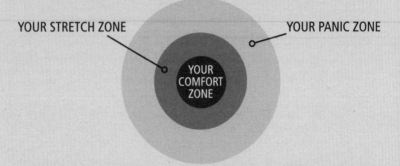

YOUR COMFORT ZONE

The stretch zone, on the other hand, represents confidence building and experience. It is the zone of awareness, personal challenge and feeling sharp. This is the zone of anticipation, preparation, planning and calculated business risk.

It is also the zone of mentoring, because a business mentor will help you to increase your area of comfort. The more time you spend in the stretch zone the bigger your comfort zone will become:

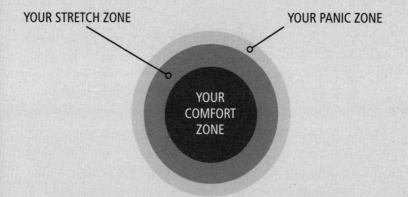

YOUR STRETCH ZONE

YOUR PANIC ZONE

YOUR
COMFORT
ZONE

Entrepreneurs and business owners will spend most of their time in the stretch zone and encourage their team and their business associates to do the same. The ideal is to achieve a productive balance between stretch and comfort, entering the panic zone only for short periods when necessary.

Understanding the stretch zone is an important part of taking decisive action and is central to the Do It! or Ditch It approach.

Chapter 2

GET THE DECISION-MAKING HABIT

*'The fine line between success and failure
depends upon the decisions that are made or
not made – every moment of every day.'*

Everybody has a process for making a decision – even though they may not realise it. In this chapter, decision-making gets personal. To what extent do your personal beliefs, values and fears influence your chances of success? What level of risk are you willing to take? Do you make decisions on your own, or do you naturally consult others?

Understanding your style of decision-making will increase your chances of creating and running a successful business – making wise decisions that work for you time and again.

Any idea can become a good idea – but not every idea is worth pursuing, nor will every business concept be commercially successful. Some people are great at generating ideas. They are like air traffic controllers in the control tower of an airport. Each great idea takes off like an aeroplane heading for a new destination. Before the first plane has a chance to land, they get another great idea. That aeroplane also takes off, heading for another new destination, and before that aeroplane lands they have another great idea – and so it goes on. This can lead to there being several metaphorical aeroplanes in the air with none of them coming in to land.

As anyone who has spent time at an airport will know, though many aeroplanes are scheduled only one can land safely per runway at a time – otherwise chaos would result. Similarly, in business, though many good ideas may be sparking your enthusiasm, the skill lies in being totally focused on landing one 'big idea' at a time – no matter how many others you have on the radar. Working through the Do It! or Ditch It approach will help to get the aeroplanes in order and land them one at a time.

That is easy to say, of course; but how can you tell which ideas are the winners, which are the losers, and when to walk away from favourite ideas that you have been developing for a very long time? The fine line between success and failure depends upon the decisions that are made or not made – every moment of every day.

RECOGNISING AN OPPORTUNITY

My philosophy is that your life is what you choose to make it. I tend to say 'yes' to new opportunities that I am keen on and often work out how to achieve them afterwards. My experience tells me that I have the skills to make things happen, and in my own life it is an approach that has worked well. However, life progression is about more than waiting for fate to play its hand – it is about creating your own destiny. Those chances are created every time we say yes or no or drift towards a decision.

'Death by indecision is one of the greatest threats to the development of a good business idea.'

WHAT IS A GOOD DECISION?

Running a business, like so much in life, depends upon a combination of knowledge and savvy, experience and application, all brought to life with a good dose of inspiration and belief. But when you are first setting up your brand new business, where exactly do you start the process? How do you decide what to do, which idea to run with and which action should become your top priority. A useful rule of thumb is always to expect the best, but plan for the worst.

'Expect the best, but plan for the worst.'

The choices you make will depend on what drives you to succeed in the first place. For some it will be the heady draw of material success, for others the desire for recognition and belonging. Some will want to create stability in their lives for themselves and their family; others will be encouraged to act by the weight of evidence in favour of success.

In many ways the criteria for selecting a good idea for a business are quite simple:

- There needs to be a big enough market to make the idea commercially viable.
- It needs to fulfil a need, a want, a desire, or solve a problem.
- The business model needs to be profitable and deliverable.
- The goods or service need to be better than those supplied by the nearest competitor.
- It needs to have a unique selling point (USP).

So far, so logical. The most important criteria for success, however, are more personal and relate to:

- Your vision for the long-term success of the idea.
- The level of excitement you feel about setting it in motion.

- The commitment you are willing to give to make it work.
- The depth of understanding you have about the market and the product or service.

And, of course, in order to launch you will need:

- A well-organised and financially sound business plan with a workable strategy.
- Enough working capital to ease cash flow, especially in the early stages.

As Warren Buffet famously said: 'Never invest in a business that you don't understand.' I would add to that: 'And never launch an idea that you don't believe in 100 per cent.'

GET THE DECISION-MAKING HABIT

Managing your business involves making decisions: lots of them. Every day. It is possible to develop a healthy decision-making habit so that you are able to make effective decisions more quickly. Get the decision-making habit by:

- **Reviewing your priorities daily.** If you know what is important you will make decisions that stay focused on the most important outcomes.
- **Learning from your mistakes.** Make sure you don't make decisions that repeat past errors.
- **Not delaying**. Do something today. If you feel tempted to delay making a decision, it is probably because you don't feel you have all the information you need to decide right now. There is no need to make an impromptu decision about something; instead, take the decision to ask someone else to provide the information or the action that you need.
- **Being flexible.** Recognise that there is usually more than one 'right way' to do things. It will enable you to delegate decisions more freely.

Strange as it may sound, not everyone makes decisions. Rather, they fall into the habit of letting other people direct their lives. Does this sound like you, or anyone you know?

Q: 'Where shall we go for dinner?'   **A:** 'I don't mind. You decide.'
Q: 'What would you like to eat?'   **A:** 'Oh, I'll have what you're having.'

The person asking the questions is forced into the decision-making role because the person answering is abdicating any kind of decision-making responsibility. In time, this can become a habit. The danger is that decision-making then becomes very stressful and difficult for the person who has the non-decision-making habit. Or, worse, they may come to feel controlled or even bullied by those around them because they have forgotten how to assert themselves.

Of course, there are other people who are more than comfortable about constantly making decisions for themselves as well as everyone else. More often than not these are the people who are comfortable taking the lead in business. (There is more about different personality types and how they interact and make decisions in Chapter 3.)

Effective decision-making means developing the skill of achieving real clarity of thought – quite quickly; and trusting your intuition to know 'this is right'. If you've got a nagging doubt that things *aren't* right, then invite your doubts up for a chat. For some people, the inner doubter or critic may be the saboteur of your dreams; for others it may be a simple matter of noticing whether your concerns are helping or hindering progress.

LISTEN TO YOUR INNER CRITIC AND CHEER ON YOUR INNER CHAMPION

Try not to resist this concept. It is a useful one. Some people push down their inner critic and try to make the most appropriate or pragmatic decision; I, on the other hand, would always encourage people to invite the inner critic in and listen to it more closely. Ask yourself, 'Where does the voice come from? Whose voice is it? Is it shouting loudly, or is it quietly nagging?' Invite every one of your doubts in for a chat and try to get to their root cause, so you can do something about them. Invite your inner champion in for a conversation, too, to counter-balance the doubter and to see whether that makes a positive difference. The role of the inner critic or doubter is to keep you safe. You may just need reassurance, or there may be a bigger issue that needs attention. In time, and with experience, the doubts will diminish and effective decision-making will happen more and more quickly.

There is a great example of the importance of paying attention to your inner critic in the film *The Glenn Miller Story*. Glenn Miller is a musician in search of a sound. In the early scenes he is really struggling with his music and he is struggling with the band. He knows things don't sound quite right, but he doesn't know what is missing – *until*, because of an injury to his trumpet player, he has to rewrite the music with the clarinet as lead instead. He hears his 'sound' for the first time. Once he has heard it, he knows without a doubt that he has found the right sound – and the Glenn Miller Orchestra takes off from that point.

Seeking the missing link within your business strategy or your marketing pitch or your team can feel similar. You intuitively know when something isn't quite right – but you don't know what it is until the right solution is found. In the meantime you have to keep searching, until everything 'clicks' into place.

MAKING IT HAPPEN

What is your reaction to the following sentences? *'Let's start at the very beginning; a very good place to start'* (Julie Andrews in *The Sound of Music*). *'Start with the end in mind'* (Stephen Covey). Does one of them appeal more than the other?

Some will be inspired by the words from *The Sound of Music*, to 'start at the very beginning', because they prefer to follow a process: getting the detail right is important to them before taking action. Others may prefer Stephen Covey's maxim that it is best to 'start with the end in mind', because the promise of the big picture and the end rewards helps us to work out what the very first step will be. I always 'start with the end in mind' and then work out what the first steps to making things happen need to be.

It is useful to know what your personal drivers are, because self-knowledge enables you to make decisions that work better for you and your business. My own approach is very simple. It depends upon asking a series of very straightforward questions: *What? Why? Where? Who? How? How much? When?*

On the basis of the answers to those questions I know whether I should take the decision forward with a 'DO IT!' or recognise that it's time to walk away and 'DITCH IT'.

By always forcing yourself to make clear decisions from the outset, and then at every step along the way, you will be more likely to reach your goals and less likely to waste precious time and resources.

Successful outcomes depend upon a sound business model, careful cash control, effective business management, favourable market forces and – importantly – passion for the idea and the decision to act. The fine line between success and failure is determined solely by the decisions we make and decisions we choose not to make, as well as personal commitment to each course of action – in every moment of every day. To succeed in business you need to develop a 'DO IT!' mindset.

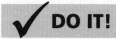 **DO IT!**

HOW TO DEVELOP A 'DO IT!' MINDSET

Success depends first and foremost on creating a solid business plan, but the eventual outcome is influenced far more by your personal motivation and your passion for the idea. The more enthusiasm you have for your project, the easier it will be for you to put in the long hours needed to make it work, and the easier it will be for you to attract funding when you need it. A backer will almost always be investing in *you* – not just your idea. They will start to judge you from the very first moment of contact. So, you need to show passion and enthusiasm for your project at all times, because you never know when you are on show.

- Surround yourself with like-minded people, who have the energy and drive to make things happen.
- Take time to read other people's success stories and books that include guidance on self-improvement. The more you fill your head with positive thoughts the more likely you are to act accordingly.
- Watch how you think. Think to yourself 'I feel great', 'I can make time' – even if you're not really feeling that way. Our thoughts influence our actions and outcomes.
- Set yourself a deadline for action for everything you do and every idea you have.

- Be decisive and stick to your decisions.
- Remain focused on the current task and bear in mind the big picture. You may have to give up short-term pleasures for the benefit of your long-term goal – but it will be worth it in the long run.
- Your passion will drive you forward with more energy than any business plan alone. If you don't feel driven to succeed you will stop before you reach your goal. Take your decisions wisely and focus only on those things you are driven to make happen.
- Think 'Can do' and ditch the 'Can't do'. At the first sign of a self-defeating negative thought, take steps to turn it around by taking a positive action.
- Believe in yourself. Only you can make your dreams and ambitions happen – no matter how well supported you are by your team and friends.

 **DITCH IT**

HOW TO OVERCOME A 'DITCH IT' MINDSET

- Ditch anything that doesn't take off within a planned time frame. It is becoming an energy stealer and will distract you from your bigger goals.
- Do not waste time regretting shoulds or might have beens. A 'Do it!' mindset focuses on the here and now.
- Watch your language. If you find yourself blaming others or circumstances, excusing yourself from blame, look again. All decisions stem from our own thoughts and actions.

It is natural to feel anxious, cautious and wary of the unknown, but our fears present us with choices. We can either let them act as a barrier to personal progress and development, or we can choose to see them as a sign that we need to take some form of action in order to stride forwards.

NAME YOUR FEARS

'Named your fear must be, before banish it you can.'

Yoda, *in* The Empire Strikes Back

I love this Yoda quote because it is wise in its observation that we all have fears and we need to understand what they are in order to break free of them and move on. When I am working with my coaching clients I invite them to reflect on possible fears or self-limiting beliefs and to ask the following questions:

- What would you attempt if you could not fail?
- What has fear cost you in the past?
- What will fear prevent you from attempting in the future?

We all know what fear feels like: the heart thumps, knees go weak, voice trembles, stomach churns and palms sweat. It's time for fight or flight. In the face of every fear we can choose whether to run away or face it with courage. Confidence doesn't develop in the absence of fear; far from it. Confidence develops from an inner belief that no matter what happens you will deal with it.

Try two more questions:

- Will you live with the regret of what might have been?

Or

- Will you take a step forward, knowing that if you give it your best you will become stronger, no matter what the outcome?

Winning the battle against fear is like strengthening a weak muscle or learning a new skill. You will gain power and knowledge over time, with practice and with patience. When you first learn to drive a car, you don't head for the motorway and hope for the best. Instead you start from a static position, simply learning what each of the controls is for. You learn to move up through the gears gradually, and gain speed slowly, safe in the knowledge that you can always put your foot firmly on the brake and come to a halt if necessary. With practice you will no longer focus on every gear change because you have learned to master the rhythm of the process. Something that you thought you might never learn suddenly becomes second nature and a lot of fun.

Fear will paralyse some people, while others need the rush of adrenalin to provide the fuel that ignites the flames of enthusiasm – providing the energy that is the driving force of success.

To banish fear and take control of your life:

1. Take time to understand what you are fearful of.
2. Ask yourself – what is the worst thing that could happen and how would you deal with it if it did?
3. Visualise success.
4. Move consciously from your comfort zone into your stretch zone – but plan your actions so that you stay out of the panic zone (see pages 22-25).

Self-limiting beliefs

Self-limiting beliefs are beliefs that limit your ability to perform well. They can take the form of negative self-talk and are often based on beliefs formed by past experiences, instincts or even cultural/family beliefs. If they are not addressed, they can really hold you back. The moment you hear yourself say 'I could never do that' or feel that something is beyond your capability before you have even tried, you are the victim of a self-limiting belief. Self-limiting beliefs can be changed one at a time by investing in personal development and learning techniques such as NLP, to build your confidence.

These techniques can help you to feel bulletproof and ready to face any challenge that may come your way. There is only one way to overcome this trait: that is to make a sincere attempt to do the very thing you thought you couldn't do. But first you will need to clear your mind of all those 'can'ts' and replace it with some 'cans'.

In the words of Yoda again:

'Do or do not. There is no try.'
Yoda, *in* The Empire Strikes Back

COMMIT TO TAKING ACTION

People who are successful in business tend to go out to meet opportunity rather than waiting for it to find them. They make active rather than reactive decisions and learn not to take the knocks too personally.

Action and inaction both determine business outcomes; both are decisions. The difference lies in the level of control that the decision-maker has over the kind of life and level of success they choose to create themselves.

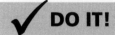 **DO IT!**

- Nurture the ideas that fire your enthusiasm and have a place in the business marketplace.
- Set goals and plan ahead so you keep up your own momentum.
- Understand your personal strengths, weaknesses, passions and fears.
- Recognise the traits you need in others.
- Create a business that will deliver successful results.

DITCH IT

- Ditch the ideas that steal time and distract from the bigger picture. Perfectionism, indecision and lack of clarity are constant threats to business success.
- Ditch personal conflict and misunderstanding and bring out the best in yourself and your associates.
- Ditch negativity and blame and transform them into self-control and personal dynamism.
- Ditch unhelpful habits and thoughts and replace them with an approach that will reinforce your successful behaviours.

If you have a great idea, commit to DO-ing it or DITCH-ing it – but don't let it stagnate or lose momentum.

'Good is good enough – crack on!'

READY, AIM ...

How to overcome procrastination

For some people, delivering the outcome is easy; the harder part is deciding when and how to get started; or which goal is the most important and what the direction of the action is going to be. If you consistently delay giving due attention to something that ought to be a priority for you or your business, you are procrastinating.

Procrastination is a time stealer and the enemy of all decision-making. You can hear it in what people say and see it in what they choose to do or not do. Their words reflect their true intentions. If you invite someone out for a drink and they reply, 'I will try ...', do you really expect them to deliver the result? The procrastinators' use of language sends them straight back towards Brain Tracy's 'Someday Isle ...' (see page xxv).

MASTERING YOUR MOTIVATION

If you ask yourself, *'What is stopping me getting started?'* your reply will probably be one or more of the following:

'I don't know what I am trying to achieve.'
'I feel bored at the thought of doing it.'
'It's not something I like doing.'
'I feel overwhelmed by the scale of the work involved.'
'I don't have the skills or knowledge to achieve it.'
'I have a self-limiting belief about my ability to achieve it.'
'It conflicts with my values.'

Instead of asking yourself a question, make a positive statement.

'I would do it now if ...'
...'I knew where I was headed.'
...'I had someone to advise me.'

...'I better understood the process involved.'
...'I had more financial information.'
...'I had the necessary skills and experience.'
...'I had confidence in my belief.'
...'It matched my values.'

'If ...' identifies the next action. 'Why?' invites you to make excuses, or tell a story. There is no story in 'if'.
Now ask yourself:

- What do I want to achieve today, this week, this year, in the long term?
- What is my primary, long-term goal?
- If I do the task in hand, what difference would it make?
- Will it take me closer to or further away from my primary goal?
- Are there aspects that I can outsource or delegate to someone who can help me achieve my primary goal more effectively?

The cure for procrastinating is goal-setting. Goal-setting drives action. Only by taking action can you bring your dreams and goals to life. Statistics tell us that only 3 per cent of the population sets and monitors personal goals. However, studies show that those individuals who set achievable goals will achieve better overall results that those who do not.

"If you D R E A M it you can DO IT!"

(Walt Disney)

Decide what you want.

Make sure it is **R**ealistic.

Stop making **E**xcuses.

Take **A**ction.

Monitor your progress.

DO IT! OR DITCH IT
DECISION-MAKING TECHNIQUE

FOCUS YOUR MIND
On a scale of 1 to 10

How we make business decisions is both individual and dependent upon circumstances. At its core, making any kind of decision really does come down to saying either 'Yes' or 'No' – to an idea, an action, behaviour, or outcome. It is also a response to a *want* or a *need*. Wants will almost always drive decisions more than needs ...

'Do I *need* this extra piece of pie?' No.

'Do I *want* it?' Yes.

'Shall I eat it?' Yes – DO IT!

At the extremes of yes or no, decision-making may be easy enough in our personal lives. 'Yes, I'd love to see that film' is a clear decision to 'Do It!' 'I hate going to that restaurant' is an equally clear decision to 'Ditch It'. However, in business, many decisions have to be made in a more objective manner; they have to take into account the long-term goal and the needs of other people. Your gut 'Yes/DO IT!' reaction may not always be the most appropriate way forward. Giving priority to what you *want* to do, rather than what you *need* to do is not necessarily a good idea. The best decision for the business and the level of priority are not always immediately clear. That is where the 1 to 10 rule becomes most helpful.

The simplest decision-making tool after 'Yes' and 'No' is to consider things on a scale of 1 to 10 (10 being 'Yes' and 1 being 'No').

'On a scale of 1 to 10 will reading this book take me closer to/further away from my goal of being able to make effective decisions?'

I hope your score will be a clear 10 and a resounding 'Do It!' but there may be many reasons why you can't answer the question yet. A lower score doesn't necessarily mean 'Ditch it'. It may just mean you need more information – or that you have a self-limiting belief about something. It can be used to assess wants and needs, facts and feelings; it can hone your priorities and help you plan your future. It is probably the most effective and instantaneous decision-making tool.

The next time you are procrastinating about what to do next, get yourself firmly back on track by asking:

'On a scale of one to ten how much closer will this action take me towards my primary goal?'

If it is not a 10, ask yourself:

'What next action will take me to a 10?'

'What is stopping me from taking the next step? (Is it money, skills, family, confidence, resources?)'

What is my greatest fear? (Is it failure, loss of face, loss of security, getting it wrong?)'

Commit to taking action:

- Decide what *is* working.
- Identify the area that isn't.
- Look at your options.
- Decide to do something about the area you have control over.

Prioritise: What is the commercial benefit to you now?

Prioritise those things that will increase revenue to your business. Make sure you are not using administrative tasks as a distraction and a way of 'being busy'.

Schedule: If not now, when?

Don't let your decisions escape. If you have identified an action, add it to your diary – and add an action date. The more you get used to doing this, the clearer your priorities will become.

Delegate: If not you, who?

Try to confine your actions to those tasks that only you can do. Outsource or delegate anything else that others can do more quickly, more cheaply and possibly more effectively than you can.

Monitor and measure: Review➔Revise➔Do It OR Ditch It

Stay in control of the process. Once you have scheduled a task or an activity, keep it under review. Revise or ditch those things that aren't working. Focus on doing only those things that truly add value to your business.

Use, 'on a scale of 1 to 10', as your barometer for taking action and you will be amazed at how much more focused your actions become.

'Don't delay. Do it today.'

Make sure that your best ideas don't die a death from indecision, and keep that momentum going once you have got things started. The Do It! or Ditch It checklists at the end of each of the eight steps in Part II, will help you to put this technique into practice.

Chapter 3

INTRODUCING THE
DISC PERSONALITIES

*'Your core values influence the way you
think, act, communicate with other people –
and make decisions.'*

Do you know how you come across to others and how you act
under pressure? This chapter introduces a simple but powerful
system for understanding how to use your core strengths to help
you succeed, and how to adapt your communication style to work
better with others in order to produce positive results and stay on
track under pressure.

DISCover whether you are naturally more **D**ominant, **I**nfluencing,
Steady or **C**ompliant, and how that influences the speed and clarity
of your decisions and your actions.

When I am recruiting for my companies, or working as a business
or leadership coach, I use a personality profiling technique (a
psychometric test) called DISC to gain an understanding of my
employees, clients and work colleagues. The DISC tool that I
prefer to use only takes seven minutes to complete but has a 95
per cent accuracy rating.

I have found DISC to be an invaluable tool for helping business
owners increase or improve self-awareness; and, from a personal

perspective, it has helped me ensure I hire right first time and, in so doing, helped me to create and maintain high-performing teams.

Completing a simple questionnaire is all it takes to obtain a DISC profile, but the self-knowledge that results will often have an immediate and profound impact on people's ability to understand, communicate and work with one another.

The modern-day DISC methodology was founded on years of research undertaken by American psychologist and inventor Dr William M. Marston (1893–1947) and others. Dr Marston also invented the lie detector machine (the polygraph).

DISC is an acronym based on four core personality groupings. Everyone will fall into one or more of the following categories. These are:

Dominant
Influencing
Steady
Compliant

Marston's DISC behavioural model classifies people primarily as either *task-orientated* or *people-orientated*, and then as either *outgoing* or *reserved*.

If you are mainly outgoing + task-orientated your style tends to be **D**
Dominant

If you are mainly outgoing + people-orientated your style tends to be **I**
Influencing

If you are mainly reserved + people-orientated your style tends to be **S**
Steady

If you are mainly reserved + task-orientated your style tends to be **C**
Compliant

OUTGOING

T **A** **S** **K**	**D** DOMINANT	**I** INFLUENCING	**P** **E** **O**
	C COMPLIANT	**S** STEADY	**P** **L** **E**

RESERVED

Dr Marston's system provides a lot of detail about the varying degrees in which people display these traits, but in *Do It! or Ditch It* I am keeping it simple and using the system to explain the four dominant traits and how they influence your leadership and decision-making abilities.

Taking a DISC questionnaire (see page 56) will help you to understand which traits apply mainly to you.

- What are your dreams and aspirations for the future? Do you immediately think on a big picture scale or do you tend to focus first on the detail? Are you fast-paced or slow-paced? Are you motivated by people or projects? Do you know what you want to achieve?
- What kind of decision-maker are you? Do you pride yourself on being decisive, impulsive, collaborative? Considered?
- What stops you making progress? Fear of failure? Fear of being judged? Insufficient facts and data? Other people's needs?
- What makes you take action? Financial reward? Personal recognition? The needs of others? A perfect outcome?
- Are you mainly people-orientated, or task-orientated? Are you concerned with facts or goals? Do you prefer to aim for short-term or long-term goals?

There are no correct or incorrect, answers but each will tell you something about your predominant business style and your preferred decision-making style.

THE D-STYLE

Outgoing + task-orientated
D-styles are Dominant, like to take action and take charge.

D-styles will solve problems and respond to challenges aggressively.

D-styles are outgoing and task-focused.

D-styles are the dominant members of the team.

Their greatest fears are being taken advantage of or failure.

Quite forcible characters, they will tell people what to do in a very direct fashion and under pressure may not be very sensitive to others' feelings.

D-styles are motivated by results, power and authority.

Well-known figures such as Oprah Winfrey, Richard Branson and Lance Armstrong are typical of High D-styles.

THE I-STYLE

Outgoing + people-orientated

I-styles are Influencers and like to interact and persuade others.

I-styles are outgoing and people-orientated.

I-styles are creative and inspirational and often flamboyant.

I-styles become active, verbal and persuasive when faced with problems.

Their greatest fears are rejection and loss of popularity. They are motivated by praise and public recognition. As managers they tend to use verbal persuasion.

I-styles like to have plenty of options.

Entertainers Billy Connolly and Jonathan Ross are typical of High I-styles, as are Whoopi Goldberg, Jim Carrey and Bill Clinton.

THE S-STYLE

Reserved + people-orientated

S-styles are Steady and like to maintain the status quo.

S-styles tend to be reserved and people-orientated.

S-styles are the steady and stable members of the team.

S-styles are supportive of others and they can often be highly sensitive.

S-styles tend to prefer an ordered pace and to start and complete one project at a time.

S-styles can be resistant to change, especially if they can see no reason for it. Their greatest fears are loss of security or change for change's sake.

S-styles may be the organisers on the team.

Princess Diana and Mother Teresa demonstrated High S-styles. Sir Paul McCartney does, too.

THE C-STYLE

Reserved + task-orientated

C-styles are Compliant and very detail-orientated.

C-styles are reserved and task-orientated.

C-styles are cautious in approach and are often highly competent.

C-styles are the analysers of the team.

C-styles may gravitate to jobs that require detail.

C-styles' greatest fears are criticism and conflict.

C-styles base their decisions on evidence and respect the official line.

C-styles like to manage by rules and regulations set by others.

The physicist Stephen Hawking and entrepreneur Bill Gates typify the High C's need for order and high standards.

HOW DISC AFFECTS BEHAVIOUR IN BUSINESS

Does the balance of the DISC characteristics mean that if you find the right four people you will have your dream team? Well, yes, in theory. Though it depends on the needs of the business. DISC is not about classifying people and putting them in a tidy box; in reality the majority of us are a mixture of more than one DISC trait. Each of us is a complex combination of personality and character traits that have been shaped by our environment. We may show one set of traits at work, and another at home. However, generally there will be some core characteristics that remain consistent in all environments – especially when under pressure.

I have found that many business leaders will often have more Dominant characteristics. The reason for this that D-style people generally don't like being told what to do, and climb the ladder of success to be masters of their own destiny. However, any personality style can run a successful business if they have the skills and desire to do so; they will just do it in a different way.

The following quotes from Richard Branson display this through a combination of both D and I traits:

'Having a personality of caring about people is important. You can't be a good leader unless you generally like people. That is how you bring out the best in them.'

'I believe in benevolent dictatorship provided I am the dictator.'

Someone like Richard Branson is likely to build a 'dream team' around him of people who are highly detailed/skilled in specific areas. This doesn't mean that he cannot do detail, but he may prefer someone else to do the research so that he can make sound decisions based on the facts presented. Interestingly, D- and I-styles, through their optimism, often look for what can go right, while S- and C-styles, through their caution, often look for what can go wrong, so having input from all four styles on your team can be really useful.

In your own business you may be great at presentations, but let yourself down with poor organisation or lack of attention to detail; you may be charismatic, but lack confidence with financial spreadsheets; you may be brilliant at what you do, but have a low tolerance for conformity and deadlines. Only you will know what you need to improve – but the important thing is to recognise the gap and to make sure you fill it.

The DISC system can be invaluable for understanding 'how people tick' because this also affects how we communicate, motivate and encourage others, which in turn has a positive effect on their performance. It also helps us to understand how and why we tend to make the decisions we do. Step 4: WHO? looks in more detail at how to create a business dream team and how to play to everyone's DISC strengths.

Before going any further, take a few moments to complete the DISCovery questionnaire online. (see page 56). You may find the results more revealing than you expected.

THE DISC APPROACH TO DECISION-MAKING

How do the DISC traits affect decision-making? What are the key personality traits to be aware of in yourself and in others? How can you use DISC to make better decisions? At the simplest level, D-styles and C-styles tend to be motivated by the 'task', whereas I-styles and S-styles are predominantly motivated by 'people'. That doesn't mean that D-styles and C-styles don't like people or that I-styles and S-styles are not good at completing tasks, but it can mean that the task-driven D-styles and C-styles are able to be less emotional about decisions than those who have more dominant, people-driven traits.

C-styles and D-styles are pragmatic and task-focused. Task-orientated decisions include:

- Deciding to 'Ditch' a non-commercial idea even though the team has committed an enormous amount of time and effort into getting it off the ground.
- Selecting the person who will get the job done, even though that person may potentially be difficult for his or her peers to work with.

I-styles and S-styles prefer to make decisions that are popular, favourable and are perceived to motivate people.

People-orientated decisions include:

- Giving an idea 'one more go' after several failures, persuaded by the team's optimism and enthusiasm.
- Selecting the person who may not have the skills but is the best 'fit' for the team on the basis that they can be trained up to do the task.

These differences will have an impact on the choice of words, leadership style and the way they announce key decisions.

The D-styles' response is likely to be decisive, straightforward and commercial. Because their greatest fear is failure, they will be willing to take tough decisions and see them through for the good of the task. They won't expect other people to take things personally – because they don't.

Ds are likely to announce decisions in a brief and direct manner that focuses on outcomes rather than the detail of how to achieve that outcome. There will be few flourishes. The language will focus on 'winning', 'delivering', being 'ahead of the competition' and 'breaking new ground'.

The I-styles' greatest fear is related to loss of popularity and a fear of rejection, so their decisions will be influenced by concerns about 'How will my decision affect the way people regard me?'

I-styles are likely to want to entertain and to win everyone over by persuasion before delivering any negative message. Decisions will be presented in an upbeat way. Bad news will be couched in terms that suggest 'this hurts me more than it does you'. Their verbal delivery is likely to be full of adverbs and adjectives. Opportunities will be 'amazing', the team will be 'extraordinary', the future will hold 'fantastic opportunities'.

The S-style's greatest fear is change (especially if they can't see any real benefits) and they are often very compassionate, so they will be concerned with how decisions will disrupt the status quo and impact on each individual. They may empathise with others to the extent where they will start to feel their pain, which can make it very tough if they are taking the lead.

S-styles are likely to focus more on the elements that will be unchanged by any decision that is being made in order to maintain stability. In the case of bad news, they will want to reassure people that their needs have been taken into account and will want to offer practical support for those who are disrupted by any changes. They will use phrases such as 'if anyone is worried', or 'there will be the least disruption possible', and will focus on the process of sincere delivery.

The C-styles may have trouble making a decision because they will want to know they have taken all the key facts into account. Their greatest fear is getting things wrong and so they can get distracted by over-analysing data until a decision makes perfect sense.

When they present the reason for a decision, C-styles are likely to include a logical argument and plenty of supporting data. There will be percentages, pros and cons and a balanced argument. They may find it harder to carry their audience as the delivery may be quite dry and fact-driven.

> People often show a combination of one, two or three DISC styles. Those who want to take a more in-depth test can do so at: www. BevJames.com. For the purposes of decision-making, look most closely at your two dominant traits.

DISCover HOW DISC CAN IMPROVE COMMUNICATION AND PRODUCTIVITY

We are all multifaceted and changeable human beings. While I have found the DISC methodology to be very reliable and useful when working with people, it is important to emphasise that the results are not a straitjacket. The DISC method enhances our understanding of ourselves and others, but the results can never predict abnormal behaviour.

For example, sometimes in life opposites attract. An outgoing person who is a High I-style may be drawn to a deep-thinking, intellectual C-style. People who marry someone opposite to themselves may then spend their time trying to make their partner more like themselves. The same can happen in business. A High D-style who likes fast decision-making and new challenges may hire an S-style person who likes efficient procedures and a slower pace. Even though the company needs both styles to deliver the end result, the D-style leader may continually put pressure on the S-style person – to encourage them to speed things up or cut corners in order to move on to the next project.

It is valuable to know what your core traits are, because the character of the person at the top of the organisation will influence the culture of the business.

When we begin to appreciate the differences and similarities in people, we stop labelling characteristics as either 'wrong' or 'right' and begin to understand them better. The DISC philosophy is 'wherever there is agreement there is power'. If we know what we need to say to others and how to adapt our tone and language in order to make them feel appreciated and understood, we can bring out the best in those we work with. If we understand what makes us react the way we do, what causes us anxiety and why we are more comfortable making certain kinds of decisions than others, our understanding will affect how we relate to others and influence the way we do business, too.

'The DISC philosophy is: Wherever there is agreement there is power.'

In each of the Do It! or Ditch It steps in Part II, you will find a list of core traits and behaviours relating to each of the DISC groups that may help or hinder the decision-making process. The eight steps show how each of these styles can be used to advantage when making decisions, and can be used to increase our options for entrepreneurial success.

DISCover WHO YOU ARE

On a short-term basis everyone can adapt their styles to suit the circumstances, and most do, depending on circumstances. The value of understanding your DISC profile is that you can consciously modify your approach when necessary.

The following pages describe the core traits of each of the DISC-style. You may find that you recognise yourself quite easily from the results of the questionnaire – but to be certain you can also take an online DISC assessment questionnaire. (Visit www. BevJames.com)

DO IT! OR DITCH IT
DECISION-MAKING TECHNIQUE
DISCover WHO YOU ARE

> The DISC method was devised following many years of rigorous research, so the version reproduced here will not be as detailed and may not be as accurate as completing a full DISC assessment. For those interested in understanding more about this fascinating and useful system, please follow the link on the Bev James website, www.bevjames.com, and take a few minutes to complete the full questionnaire.

1. Below are nine rows of four words. Using the numbers 1, 2, 3, 4, categorise each of the words in each horizontal row.
    1 = least like you; 4 = most like you. Use each number once in each row.

2. Try to complete the task based on your immediate reaction.

3. Give yourself no more than 5 minutes to complete the questionnaire.

4. Once you have finished, add up the totals in each vertical column.

COLUMN 1		COLUMN 2		COLUMN 3		COLUMN 4	
Directing		Influencing		Steady		Cautious	
Self-certain		Optimistic		Deliberate		Restrained	
Adventurous		Enthusiastic		Predictable		Logical	
Decisive		Open		Patient		Analytical	
Daring		Impulsive		Stabilising		Precise	
Competitive		Persuading		Accommodating		Curious	
Assertive		Talkative		Modest		Tactful	
Experimenting		Charming		Easy-going		Consistent	
Forceful		Positive		Sincere		Perfectionist	
TOTAL		TOTAL		TOTAL		TOTAL	

NEXT:

5. Circle the number in the DISC columns that most closely match your totals:

Column 1 → **D** Dominant

Column 2 → **I** Influencing

Column 3 → **S** Steady

Column 4 → **C** Compliant

D	I	S	C
40	40	40	40
38	38	38	38
36	36	36	36
34	34	34	34
32	32	32	32
30	30	30	30
28	28	28	28
26	26	26	26
24	24	24	24
22	22	22	22
20	20	20	20
18	18	18	18
16	16	16	16
14	14	14	14
12	12	12	12
10	10	10	10

WHAT'S YOUR STYLE?

The result will give you greater insights as you read the rest of the book and will help you to discover your natural style and how it changes under pressure.

The column with the highest score is your most pronounced style; the column with the lowest score is your least pronounced style.

A very high score of 34–40 suggests that you strongly share the characteristics of that style. In some places in the book I refer to High Ds, High Is, High Ss, High Cs. This means you.

A low-end score in the region of 10–16 suggests that the style is less pronounced and takes a different form. In some places in the book I refer to Low D-styles, Low I-styles, Low S-styles, Low C-styles. This means you.

Any score above the bold line in the table above suggests you err towards a pronounced style. You may also find that your scores change when you are under pressure. For example, you may feel more inclined to lead and your D-style will increase; you may find you are less likely to check your facts before you act, and take more risks, so your C-style decreases. You may also find that the balance of your scores changes subtly if you consider your traits in a home or social environment.

Whichever trait scores the highest amount is your dominant trait. The next highest is your secondary trait. For example, my result is High D/I.

YOUR RESULT

D   DOMINANT

'DOMINANT Ds' are people who like to take action

Dominant traits relate to how a person solves problems and responds to challenges.

They are:	Outgoing and task-focused
They tend to be:	Dominant, direct, demanding, decisive, determined
High D-styles	Are decisive and forthright when overcoming problems
	May be quick to anger or show intolerance
Low D-styles	Feel less need to take control from a dominant position. Are slower to anger and are more tolerant
Greatest fears:	Being taken advantage of, failure
Motivated by:	Power and authority
Management style:	Directing
Communication style:	Tell people in a direct fashion
Method of control:	Force of character
Core business trait:	Drive for results

Decision-making style: Fast and decisive

DOMINANT COMBINATIONS

If you find that more than one trait prevails, you will have a combination style:

D-style with I-style
A driven people person
- A decisive person who has a combination of directness and persuasion.
- Prefers to be in a position of authority and seeks personal challenges.

- Leads people with a combination of 'telling' (directness) and 'selling' (persuasiveness).
- Will accomplish goals through people.
- Outgoing – loves activity. Is purposeful, productive, a promoter.
- Thrives on challenge. Is a motivator of people and a convincing, persuasive debater.
- Can be opinionated, impetuous and manipulative.

D-style with S-style
A driver with a stabilising force

- Can often suffer internal conflict with the D wanting to change and the S wanting to remain the same.
- Will want to see things through to completion – preferably one at a time.
- Leads people with a combination of directness and thoughtfulness.
- Can fluctuate between tolerance and intolerance of poor performance.
- Will consider the impact of decisions on others.

D-style with C-style
Forceful and analytical

- Wants things done now and done correctly.
- May come across as a little 'cool' interpersonally.
- Very task-orientated.
- Acts positively and directly when challenged. A forceful individual, who will take a stand and fight for their position.
- Willing to take calculated risks, but may oscillate between driving forwards and putting on the brakes.
- Likes goals and details. A leader who is decisive but requires detail.

I   INFLUENCING

'INFLUENCING Is' are people who like to interact and persuade others

Influencer traits relate to how a person tries to persuade others.

They are:	Outgoing and people-orientated
They tend to be:	Inspirational, influential, impulsive, interested in people
High I-style	Becomes active, verbal and persuasive when faced with problems. Responds actively to challenges and may try to reach an agreement. Are joyful and optimistic
Low I-style	Uses data and facts and has a tendency to be more non-verbal. Tends towards pessimism
Greatest fears:	Rejection, loss of popularity
Motivated by:	Praise and recognition
Management style:	Motivating/inspirational
Communication style:	Sells
Method of control:	Verbal persuasion
Core business trait:	Working well with people; generating enthusiasm

Decision-making style: Prefers to have options

INFLUENCING COMBINATIONS

If you find that more than one trait prevails, you will have a combination style:

I-style with D-style
Charismatic and direct
- Strives to establish rapport with others immediately on meeting and may be charming.

- Accomplishes goals through people. Is highly productive.
- Likes to inspire others to achieve.
- Positive and persuasive.
- Outgoing; enthusiastic; possesses charisma and has great resolve.
- May talk too much. Is complimentary.
- May be over-optimistic.

I-style with S-style

A thoughtful, positive person

- A good listener and talkative.
- Likes to be with positive people.
- Seeks to be liked and popular.
- Has optimism tempered with a degree of caution.
- Tries to win people over through persuasion and emotional appeal.
- As a leader, may be too permissive of poor performance.
- May lack follow-through.

I-style with C-style

A creative planner

- Sociable but self-reliant.
- Strives to win people over with persuasion and tact
- Likes to get 'buy in' from team members.
- Cautiously optimistic.
- Emotional and creative.
- Will promote other people and projects.

S   STEADY

'STEADY Ss' are people who like to maintain the status quo

They are:	Reserved and people-orientated
They tend to be:	Steady, stable, supportive, sensitive
High S-style	Tends to prefer a slow pace and prefers to start and complete one project at a time. They are quite resistant to change. Under pressure they may become passive/aggressive in response and prefer not to stand out from the crowd. It is quite hard to read their emotions
Low S-style	Prefers a faster pace and has a greater desire for change. They can be very emotionally expressive
Greatest fears:	Loss of security, change
Motivated by:	Security
Management style:	Organisers
Communication style:	Listening
Method of control:	Slowing down
Core business trait:	Service and support
Decision-making style:	**Systems and process**

STEADY COMBINATIONS

If you find that more than one trait prevails, you will have a combination style:

S-style with D-style

A stabilising manager

- Can have internal conflict between risk and the need for safety.
- Prefers to deal with one assignment at a time.
- Strives to stabilise their environment.

- Can be active and thorough.
- Often has internal conflict with the D wanting change and the S wanting the status quo.
- In management, can be too permissive of poor performance.

S-style with I-style
A people person
- Likes to talk and likes to listen – a great socialiser.
- Easy-going, diplomatic and sociable.
- Will try to persuade and 'sell' rather than be direct and 'tell'.
- In management, may be reluctant to take unpopular decisions.
- Will make popular decisions quickly.

S-style with C-style
Steady and systematic
- Likes to work at their own pace.
- Will prefer an accurate job 'brief'.
- Will like to work with systems and procedures.
- Will prefer to see things through to completion one at a time.
- Will have a balance of people skills and task tendencies.
- Will be more reserved in nature.

C   COMPLIANT

'COMPLIANT Cs' are people who respond to rules and regulations

They are:	Reserved and task-orientated
They tend to be:	Cautious, calculating, competent, compliant, contemplative, careful
High C-style	Prefers to comply with rules set by others. Under pressure will respond passively/ aggressively and seek to justify their actions. They are cautious in approach and will use analysis to decide whether to move forward
Low C-style	Will challenge rules and seek independence. They are more fearless
Greatest fears:	Criticism, conflict
Motivated by:	Systems and procedures
Management style:	Rule enforcement
Communication style	Writes
Method of control:	Information
Core business trait:	Quality and standards
Decision-making style:	**Based on evidence**

COMPLIANT COMBINATIONS

If you find that more than one trait prevails, you will have a combination style:

C-style with D-style
Systematic and task-focused

- Will manage by the rule book.
- May appear a little interpersonally 'cool'.
- May stick strictly to policy and may appear rigid in following rules and regulations.

- Wants tasks to be completed accurately and quickly.
- Can be difficult to get along with because they may put the needs of the task ahead of the needs of people.
- Can be overly self-critical.

C-style with I-style
An analytical communicator
- Has a balance between persuasiveness and logic.
- Makes decisions based on proven precedent and known facts.
- Will persuade others to follow rules.
- May have conflict when dealing with unpopular decisions.
- Can articulate data with great effectiveness.
- Can be gifted communicators.
- Can suffer from big mood swings; highly emotional; analyses things too much; critical; often rigid; may have a poor sense of self.

C-style with S-style
A thoughtful analyst
- A more reserved individual.
- Has a combination of task and people skills.
- Will want time to see things accurately through to completion.
- Exhibits a precise, detailed, stable nature.
- Systematic thinkers.
- Often tactful, diplomatic manner and would prefer to avoid antagonism.

Chapter 4

WHAT IS YOUR LEADERSHIP STYLE?

'No matter how excellent you are at what you do – it is the thing that you don't do as well that will give your competitors an advantage and threaten your future success.'

Running a business is about more than having a great idea. It is about taking responsibility, and being consistently one step ahead of the game. Success depends upon self-knowledge. What drives you to act? How do you communicate? How do you prefer to work? Are you a leader or a follower? Do you use your initiative or wait for things to happen? What is your natural management style?

Entrepreneurs and business leaders have many traits in common. They tend to be ambitious, impatient, excited by competition, lead from the front, and they are motivated by a passion for what they do and a desire for profit and success. To succeed in business, leaders and managers need to be mentally resilient, with the ability to motivate others, especially when the going gets tough. But each business person is an individual, too, and in reality few people can say they have all these traits in equal measure.

To make a success of what you do, it is important to have a realistic understanding of your strengths – the things that you are good at and you enjoy; and your weak spots – those areas you find more of a challenge. This kind of self-knowledge is vital for your future success. Your business is only as strong as the strongest of your weak spots. Your weak spots are not negative traits, they are simply 'lesser strengths' in a business context. They are those skills that you do not enjoy as much or that you carry out less consistently.

For example, you may find inspiring people easy, but find it hard to discipline them if they have done a poor job; you may see clearly how to 'get the job done' fast but have a low capacity for checking detail. In order to be a success, you need to play to your strengths – and to know how and when to raise your game – and when to partner with others who have the skills you need.

We also have undiscovered talents: those areas that are untested, which are opportunities for personal growth and further strengths to be developed. Neglecting your personal weaknesses can expose real threats to your business. If you are aware of those threats in advance you can plan to accommodate and overcome them.

> *'In order to be a success, you need to play to your strengths – and to know how and when to raise your game – and when to partner with others who have the skills you need.'*

Together, your Strengths, Weak Spots, Opportunities and Threats can be assessed as part of a personal SWOT check. A SWOT check can be a fast and extremely useful way to do a skills check, to help you to keep your strengths and weaknesses in mind and to achieve ongoing development. This is usually laid out in a grid format.

See page 77 for guidance on how to use the SWOT spot.

LEADING FROM THE FRONT

An important part of being an effective business leader is the willingness to take responsibility. This means in part being able to weigh up options and have the strength of character to make the best possible decision quite quickly. The characteristic that I have noticed consistently when working with successful people is that they are ready to be accountable for things that go wrong and they don't dwell on past mistakes.

When you take personal responsibility you put yourself in control and are able to influence the future outcome of a situation. If, on the other hand, you are consistently looking for someone else to blame, you make yourself a victim of circumstance and other people's decision-making.

It is a powerful strategy when managing other people, too. If you have a tendency to want to take back control or to protect others from the impact of making a mistake – think again. We all learn by doing. Support your staff; coach them; but enable them to correct their own errors so that they will be less likely to make the same mistake again. They will also gain personal satisfaction from knowing they have the ability to complete the task effectively. The leader is ultimately responsible – but the team member is accountable for their actions within their area of control. (Managing people is part of the all-important Step 4: WHO? in the Do It! or Ditch It eight-step decision-making process. See page 154.)

Jamie Constable is a venture capitalist and founder and owner of RCapital. RCapital owns the Little Chef roadside restaurant chain and fourteen other companies. I have an enormous amount of respect for Jamie's calm demeanour and laser-like ability to spot a business opportunity and make sound financial decisions. We are on the board of two companies together and he is a big influence on my own business life. I asked Jamie how he manages to cope when things don't go to plan. He says his strategy is not to dwell on the problem.

'If I can't influence it I don't spend time worrying about it, there's no point,' he says.

It is a good piece of advice. Focus your attention on the things that are within your sphere of influence and work to increase the range of that influence. Clarity of thought is what you need to succeed.

DEVELOPING SELF-AWARENESS WILL STRENGTHEN YOUR LEADERSHIP SKILLS

Self-awareness is an essential skill for a successful leader to develop, because the way we view ourselves is not always how others see us. You may see yourself as focused and direct, or serious and in control, whereas others may experience your attitude as contradictory or controlling. Being aware of your strengths and weaknesses and how you come across to others – especially when under pressure – can make all the difference when motivating a team to perform well and positively. If you know where your weak points are you can compensate for them and build a team around you who may be stronger than you in core areas. Every time you take on someone new, employ them with a space on your dream team in mind, so that you gradually acquire all the business skills your company needs.

HOW TO BUILD A TEAM OF SHINING STARS

If all your team were shining stars, how would that impact on the bottom line of the business? Some years ago I took over a business and a team of seventeen, which included several passengers. I reduced it to a team of nine, all of whom are still with me today and who help me to run all my businesses. They remain far more productive than the team of seventeen.

It's not just the people on the pitch who matter – it's the people behind them. The way to encourage your team of potential stars to become shining stars is to improve your own communication and decision-making. The clearer and more respectful you are, the greater your influence will be and the more confident and effective they will become.

Being aware of your own strengths and weaknesses and your personal leadership style will help you to make decisions about recruitment criteria and who you have in which role.

Using the DISC model – from the top down

In a manufacturing company, Judy, a team leader, is S-style (Steady). One of her junior team members, Chris, is D-style (Dominant). The need for the S-style to avoid conflict and the D-style to be quite vocally challenging can make it difficult for Judy as the manager to approach Chris when he is in a bad mood.

However, in this company respectful communication is one of the key criteria for personnel selection. Therefore, it becomes possible for Judy to tackle Chris's moodiness in a behaviour-focused rather than a personal way, by saying:

'Today, when you raised your voice you came across quite aggressively and the atmosphere in the department became quite tense as a consequence. You know our philosophy. That that kind of attitude is not acceptable as it impacts on everyone. If you are feeling annoyed in future, please come and speak to me personally.'

Deciding to act immediately to nip awkward situations in the bud is usually the most effective way to contain such a situation. It is always easier to have a conversation if the boundaries have already been put in place.

Using the DISC model – from the bottom up

The DISC principles can also have an impact on how members of the team at the lower level are able to talk to their manager.

Jean and her team were DISC-profiled. Jean was DS, which meant she could swing from being a risk taker to being very cautious. She was head of a large sales team. She would frequently get into D-mode to take a risky but potentially profitable business decision, which would then trigger her anxiety and the need for S-style security. In panicking that she might have taken too much of a risk, she would take action in go-getting D-style again – at which point she could become very domineering, making unreasonable demands on her team. 'Why didn't you say this?' 'Why didn't you say that?' She would bark, freezing the mood in the open-plan office. They wanted her out of the way and in a room on her own.

One day she was being particularly picky when she was approached by her PA, Robin, who had been nominated by the rest of the department to say something. Robin was profiled as a C-style person, very task-orientated but conflict-averse.

'Jean,' she said, 'we need to hit target today. We know we'll do it, but you're making us feel really jangled. Your "D" is off the clock. We need you to go and work from home today. We are going to hit target, and I will call you when we have done it.'

The DISC approach allowed the soft C to approach the scary D and tackle the problem in a non-combative way. Jean laughed, understood and went home. Though what they were really saying is, 'You're being domineering and aggressive today.'

Self-awareness is brand awareness

You are your company; more than that, you are your brand. The newer the company, the more aware you need to be that everything you do impacts on your immediate reputation and your future success.

'In the context of work, what is important to me?'
'How do I want to be perceived by my customers or clients?'
'What are my values?'
'How do I want to be regarded by my work colleagues when they're talking to friends and family?'

You may think you know what is important to you and, of course, you make decisions based on your values every single day. But unless you take time to think about them and write them down you are likely to be acting on instinct, which means you may not communicate your message effectively to those around you. If you don't understand yourself, you won't recognise your blind spots, and you will leave yourself and your business vulnerable.

Be true to your values

What are the things that are important to you? What are your core values? It is important to know, because you will work at your best when your values, your decisions and your actions are aligned. Health and fitness may be of major importance to you, but when was the last time you exercised or reined in your eating habits?

Respect may rank high on your list of values, but what does that really mean in terms of running your business? Do you show respect for your customers' needs or your clients' time? Do you speak respectfully to your team? Do you treat yourself and your family with consistent respect? Perhaps you have a passion for the environment. Take a look at the way you are running your business. Are you using sustainable resources at work?

Time to think

Give yourself some thinking time to work out which values play a part in your vision for your business – and consider how you display and live those values every day. There is a difference between the things you need and the things you feel you ought to care about – and those you truly value. Look at your work-based values; consider how and whether you actually live those values and decide how you want to demonstrate those values on a daily basis.

Remain flexible

In the current marketplace, business owners need to remain flexible in their decision-making and alert to the need to change or adapt their business model in line with the changing way that consumers buy goods and services. For example, Internet shopping and the speed of development in digital technology are evolving at such a rate that it is no longer possible to plan a business and know with certainty that the commercial model will be valid for more than a year or two. The longevity of many businesses and services in their traditional form is under constant pressure.

Invest in self-development

In the last ten years I have developed a whole series of businesses. Along the way I have invested tens of thousands of pounds in different training courses and other forms of personal development; it is a principle that I would recommend highly to everyone who is an owner-manager. People think nothing of investing in new technology or training new staff – but they rarely acknowledge that they have a skills gap themselves.

Personal training for you as the business *owner* is a must as part of your annual budget. Being aware of what you don't know and taking steps to fill in that knowledge gap – to turn them into opportunities for personal growth and development – is probably the most important key to success that there is.

> *'Being aware of what you don't know and taking steps to fill in that knowledge gap ... is probably the most important key to success that there is.'*

DO IT! OR DITCH IT

DECISION-MAKING TECHNIQUE

REVIEW THE SWOT SPOT

Dun & Bradstreet report that the number one reason that businesses go bust is due to a lack of business knowledge or the skills of the business owner. With an estimated 50 per cent of businesses expected to go bust in their first year, and 95 per cent to cease trading within the first five years, who can afford not to take the situation seriously?

> *'The number one reason that businesses go bust is due to a lack of business knowledge or the skills of the business owner.'*

HOW MUCH SWOTTING DO YOU DO?

When I work with business owners, I recommend that they initially conduct a SWOT analysis. SWOT is an acronym for:

Strengths
Weaknesses
Opportunities
Threats

There are two types of SWOT that I recommend: one for the analysis of *their business* and one for the analysis of *themselves*.

A SWOT can be done very quickly as a way of assessing whether to Do or Ditch an idea immediately; or it can be done with a great deal more thought and preparation as an essential step in your business and personal planning process.

Draw a large box and divide it into four equal sections, by drawing two lines: one horizontally across the middle and another vertically, from top to bottom. Write one of the letters S, W, O, T in the corner of each section. You are now ready to begin a SWOT analysis for you and/or your business.

THE BUSINESS SWOT ANALYSIS

The business SWOT is designed to evaluate your business in relation to your competitors and the market generally. Ask yourself:

'What's really important to me about my business (or my business idea)?'
'What do I think the business does well?'
'What do our customers say we do really well?'
'What could it be better at?'
'Where is it losing out to competitors?'

Strengths
In this box, list what you feel your business is good at, and what you feel makes it better than your competitors.

Weaknesses
In this box you will need to list the challenge areas you may have within the business.

Opportunities
In this box you will need to list the things you can do to improve upon your challenge areas within the business.

Threats
In this box you will need to itemise anything that may restrict your business growth, development, or success, if not addressed.

S

What resources does your business have?

Do you have a strong brand or reputation?

Do you have a particular expertise?

What want/need does your business offer/solve?

What key personnel are in your business?

Who are the top performers within your business?

Do you have strong systems/procedures (lead-generation, sales, follow-up strategies)?

W

What limits your business growth (finance, skills, machinery, personnel)?

Is your perceived reputation solid?

Is your brand strong enough?

Is there a perception that your business/ product gives value/ reliability?

Do competitors have the edge?

Do you lack expertise in any area?

Are your team self-motivated?

Do your team care about the business/ clients?

Is there a negative culture within the workforce?

Is the location of your business good?

O

Are there untapped networking opportunities?

Are there developing markets that you are aware of (internet, overseas)?

Are there any new products or services about to launch?

Are there any mergers, joint ventures or strategic alliances that would strengthen the position of your business?

Are there any changes in legislation that could be advantageous?

T

Do you rely on certain individuals too much?

Do one or more team member/s hold valuable information in their head?

Might key team members join the competition?

Is your database secure?

Are there any forthcoming changes in legislation that may affect your business?

Is your business under threat from competitors?

Do you foresee any financial/cash flow difficulties?

Do you rely on one or a limited number of customers?

What obstacles does your business currently face?

THE PERSONAL SWOT ANALYSIS

The Personal SWOT analysis is designed to evaluate your strengths and weaknesses in relation to your ambitions and potential. Ask yourself:

Strengths
In this box, list what you feel you are good at and the skills you would like to strenghten. Don't be modest or shy about this part.

Weaknesses
In this box, list your weak spots and areas that are a challenge. These are the areas you would like to address and overcome.
Don't worry – you haven't got to show them to anyone else.

Opportunities
In this box you will need to list the things you can do to improve your skills further and overcome your challenge areas to develop yourself for the future.

Threats
In this box you will need to itemise anything that may restrict your development if unaddressed.

S	W
What experience (or qualifications) do you have?	What do you avoid doing?
What skills do you possess?	What limits you?
What do you think you do better than anyone else?	What fears do you have (conflict, failure)?
What influential contacts do you have?	What skills do you lack?
What achievement are you most proud of?	What knowledge do you lack?
What are the strong points about your character/personality?	What personality traits hold you back?
	What vulnerabilities do you have (health, finance, relationship)?
	What negative traits do you have (easily stressed, quick to anger)?
	What might those around you see as a weakness?
O	**T**
Are there any courses you can attend?	What obstacles might limit your personal progress/development?
Are there any self-development programmes?	Could any of your weaknesses lead to threats if not addressed?
Do you know someone who can be a mentor?	What lack of skill or ability holds you back?
Is there a coach who could help you develop?	What self-limiting belief holds you back?
Do any of your current strengths open any doors/make you even more useful?	

Recognising your own strengths and weaknesses before you start recruiting or outsourcing will help you to make the right hiring decisions – and will also enable you to build a team that will get the job done effectively when they are working together.

The following tips were recommended to me by a leading business strategist. They have often kept me on track and work very well in relation to reviewing the SWOT spot.

Ask yourself the following questions in relation to your Strengths, Weaknesses, Opportunities and Threats:

What do you need to START doing?

Take action? Set achievable goals? Monitor your progress? Seek advice? Get a mentor?

What do you need to STOP doing?

Procrastinating? Living in the past? Having regrets? Blaming others? Putting yourself down?

What do you need to do LESS of?

Spending? Watching TV? Eating junk food? Putting everyone else's needs ahead of your own?

What do you need to do MORE of?

Networking? Saving money? Planning? Monitoring cash flow? Taking action?

A SWOT analysis can be as instant or as in-depth as it needs to be. It is the ideal partner to the 1 to 10 rule on page 41.

Chapter 5

WHERE ARE YOU HEADING?

'Understand what you need to do and how you need to be in order to have the outcome you want.

In order to know where you are heading, you first have to know what you need and what you want. Every decision we make and everything we achieve begins in the mind.

To achieve anything in life we need to adopt the right behaviours. Everything we *Do* is influenced by who we want to *Be* or think we are, and what we want to *Have*. Those behaviours start in the mind, where what we think affects what we feel, which influences our actions each and every day. To *Have* what you want in business and in the rest of life, you must understand what you need to *Do* and *Be* differently, in order to *Have* the outcome you want.

Do → Be → Have

It sounds simple, but many people make the majority of their decisions based on what other people want and need, rather than their own desires. As a result it can sometimes be hard to know what you really think and feel – or what you truly want to achieve.

DON'T SET YOUR GOALS *IN* THE FUTURE – SET THEM *FROM* THE FUTURE

To help people to determine their business goals, I like to encourage them to look both *backwards* and *forwards* to their future before focusing on what they need to do in the present to make their future dream a reality. By adjusting our thinking so that we are living as if our future is happening NOW, we gradually change our thought processes and expectations. We learn to adapt the decisions that we make on a daily basis to those that are more likely to make the goal a reality. My method for achieving this is to invite people to imagine they are entering a virtual time machine. This technique can be used in many aspects of life, including personal and business.

This is a very powerful exercise to use in business decision-making. Use it to focus on what you need to Do next – in order to Be the way you want to be – and in order to Have the outcomes you are visualising for the future. See page 86 for step-by-step guidelines on how to apply it.

GET CLEAR

Many goals are not achieved because they are too vague. Clarity is the key to success. You need to know what you want and why you want it. 'I want to have business premises next year' is unlikely to become a reality. Other questions need to be asked to gain clarity: Why? Where? When? For how much? What are your specifications?

GET PLANNING

Dreams will only become reality if you take steps to turn them into practical actions. Taking action involves time and planning:

but it takes no more time to plan a big outcome than it does a small one. So, when you are mapping out your vision, make it as wide and broad as you can imagine it to be. See how large your comfort zone is at present and where it might extend to in the future. Decide where you are aiming for now – but keep your future possibilities in view, too. You might begin with a market stall but have in mind a chain of offices across Asia and Australia. Anything is possible if you begin to live as if your future is happening right now.

Change the reminders over time so that they are always current and reflect the true nature of your ambitions. As the saying goes: 'Be careful what you wish for – you might just get it!'

> *'Reach for the moon and you may land among the stars.'*
>
> Jackie Gleason

TELL YOUR STORY

Feel-good stories often start with 'Once upon a time ...' The future is always rich with possibility and your time can be filled with anything you choose. Imagine you are being interviewed after achieving your goal. The interviewer asks you how you did it. What attitudes and behaviours contributed to your success?

NOW IT'S TIME TO GET STARTED ...

DO IT! OR DITCH IT
DECISION-MAKING TECHNIQUE
LOOK BACK FROM THE FUTURE

Use the focus of this exercise to focus on what you need to do next – in order to be the way you want to be and – in order to have the outcomes you are visualising for the future.

You are now in your time machine. Are you sitting comfortably? It is time to begin.

LOOK TO THE PAST

Imagine yourself going back five years, and then ask yourself:
'How would I have introduced myself five years ago?'
'Where am I living?'
'Who am I living with?'
'What are my hobbies?'
'Who are my friends?'
'Where am I working?'
'What am I earning?'
'What is my role?'
'What am I good at?'
'What would I like to be better at?'
'What are my ambitions?'
'What do I want to do/be/have in five years time?'

For example:
'My name is Tom. I am 22. I live in a rented flat by the river with girlfriend, Grace. My hobbies are cycling and photography. I

am an employee with an IT company, earning £15,000 a year. I am good at photography and I really enjoy it. I take photos for friends' weddings and sell my prints online in my spare time. My ambition is to run my own photographic business. In five years' time I would like to be earning £50,000 a year and have my own home and family.'

This useful first step helps people to see the difference between their aspirations and their present reality. They are able to reconnect with their ideals and their ambitions – and to reflect on where their choices have led them.

LOOK TO THE FUTURE

After pausing to take stock in the present, I then invite them to travel forwards in time, to five years into the future. This is the aspirational part of the exercise. I ask them to think BIG. How do you want your life to look in five years' time? Just how great do you want your future to be?

Ask yourself:
  'How will I introduce myself in five years' time?'
  'Where am I living?'
  'Who am I living with?'
  'What is my lifestyle?'
  'What am I known for?'
  'What am I enjoying?'
  'Who am I associating with?'
  'Do I own any properties?'
  'What are my luxuries?'
  'What do I need to be better at?'
  'How are things different from ten years ago?'
  'What important decisions have I made?'
  'Is there anything that I would like to do/be/have in the next five years?

For example:

> 'My name is Tom, I am married to a lovely lady and we are planning to start a family. I own a rooftop flat in Chelsea that was paid for from my photographic contracts with sports manufacturers and my online photo library. I hardly recognise the person I used to be. In five years' time I see myself running a state-of-the-art photographic studio that provides facilities and training for up-and-coming photographers, and have made enough money to be able to free up time to spend with my family. Oh yes – I own a beach home in southern Italy and a Ducati motorcycle, too.'

For some people the aims will be value-driven and idealistic; for others, material gain or status will be important; and others will want to improve their skills and competence. There are no right or wrong answers – this is simply a powerful way to encourage yourself to think about and really focus on what you want to have achieved in your future.

In Tom's case, there are some enormous financial differences between his aspirations and his present situation. He will need to make some tough and focused decisions over the years ahead if he really wants to achieve his dreams.

LOOK AT THE PRESENT

Now step back inside that time machine and think back from the future to the first thing you did that set you on the right track towards your goal. What was it? Be very clear and precise about it and see yourself doing it. Begin it *now* and take the first step into a future you can be proud of by asking yourself ten key questions:

TEN QUESTIONS TO FOCUS ON YOUR FUTURE DECISIONS IN THE PRESENT

1. What decision would make the biggest difference to your business life right now?

Whether you are an employee, a start-up entrepreneur or an established business owner, you probably wish there were more hours in the day. Investing money or resources in outsourcing, training or mentoring can be an excellent way to free yourself up to focus on the elements of your business that need your unique skills and vision.

2. If you stay on your current path, where will you end up?

Is your business heading in the direction you want it to? What is making you money? Where are you losing money? What activities contribute to the growth of your business? How can you spend your time most effectively? Take ten minutes to plan your day first thing in the morning, and make sure you are not busy being busy.

3. What are you tolerating or putting up with?

Most people are 'putting up with' something that they feel would be too time-consuming to sort out. It might be your terms of business, an awkward client relationship, a poorly designed website or an underproductive member of staff. Whatever it is, a point will come where there will be a cost involved in putting off the moment of decision.

4. If you could improve one business relationship who would it be with, and why?

It is a truism in business that 80 per cent of your profits come from 20 per cent of your contacts. Do you know who your most valuable business contacts are? There is another line that goes, keep your friends close and your enemies closer. Could any of your relationships be causing your business damage? Do you need to make time to build some business bridges?

5. What are you putting off doing and what will it cost you if you don't do it?

This may be connected to your answer to question number three; or it may be connected to a personal skills gap or a lack of knowledge. If you are stuck in your comfort zone, sooner or later there will be a cost involved. Is now the time to grasp the nettle and to plan for change?

6. How different would your life be if you followed through with this goal?

Developing your skills in, for example, public speaking, market research, social media, financial planning or people management can transform your ability to achieve your dreams. Investing time in yourself as well as your business will develop your range of skills and turbo-charge your drive and your business.

7. What will you regret not doing with your business life in later years?

Few of us give ourselves enough time to reflect on the whole life picture. A common business coaching exercise invites people to write their own obituary, highlighting past and future achievements. This is 'starting with the end in mind' in a very real sense and can wake people up to the time they have left to achieve their true goals.

8. What has lack of confidence or self-belief stopped you achieving?

Everyone has self-limiting beliefs of some sort. I once had a self-limiting belief about being able to talk to large groups of people; now I am not fazed if I need to speak to a thousand people. If your beliefs are getting in your way, you can choose to make time to take advice and get out of your own way.

9. What is your purpose? What elements of your business are you passionate about?
If you identify your true purpose you can plan every decision to take you closer to achieving your goal. Every choice you make – from actions and reactions to promises and excuses – provides clear clues as to where your true motivation and priorities lie. There is little point in building a business around something you feel is a good idea if every time you are faced with a time choice you are diverted into doing something else.

10. What is the one change you could make that would make you feel happier about the way you run your business?
Every change begins with a single step. What one thing would make a difference to the future of your business, now?

'Get ready to Do It! – and get started, right now.'

PART II

TURN IDEAS INTO ACTION AND MAKE DECISIONS THAT COUNT

Eight steps to business success

STEP 1: WHAT?

What's the big idea?

EVALUATION

'If everyone is thinking alike, then someone isn't thinking.'
General George S. Patton

Step 1: WHAT? focuses on the decisions you make during the evaluation stage: assessing and deciding which ideas to develop and which to walk away from.

In theory there is no such thing as a bad idea, just an idea whose time has not yet come. Nevertheless, not every idea is commercially viable and few are completely original. Most 'new' ideas will improve on an existing idea or service, which means there will be plenty of research and experience to draw upon when testing the concept.

Beware the danger zone: the evaluation stage is not so much about perfecting your product or service – you can do that later – it is about identifying what is unique about what you have to offer, and whether there are people out there who want and need it. Most business decisions need to be financially driven and they need to maintain their pace. The Do It! or Ditch It approach encourages you to take action promptly, so that you can assess what is working, and to ditch decisively, so that you don't waste precious time and energy on those things that are 'nice to have' but won't take you where you want to go.

People often ask me how they can be sure that their business idea is failsafe. The truth is, you can't be sure. Every new business is a learning curve. The early stages of starting up a business are full of excitement and potential. You may feel energised and anxious in equal measure. You are likely to have high expectations for the future. This is also the stage at which you are most vulnerable and liable to make expensive mistakes. The decisions you make at the evaluation stage can determine the later profitability of your business.

Ideas are two a penny. Deciding which one to act upon is the challenge. One of the common pitfalls is spending too much time on evaluating the product or service and not enough time on deciding how to market and distribute it. Time and time again I see examples of this: the person who designs an IT product, but extends the evaluation stage to the point where it becomes obsolete before launch; the author who has self-published a book, but hasn't found a way to distribute it; the trainer who has a course, but no one to sell it to; a designer who has invested in a clothing range, but hasn't asked for buyer feedback before setting the price point.

TIMES ARE CHANGING

Markets change, trends come and go and customers' needs evolve. An awareness of what your customers want and need is fundamental to commercial decision-making, and it is important to test and evaluate your assumptions at every stage. Ask yourself:

'Is there a genuine opportunity here?'
'How much do I believe in the idea?'
'Can I sell it?'
'Do I know the market well enough to launch?'

In the digital age, today's big idea may well become tomorrow's old news – *fast*. The look of the typical high street is changing rapidly as long-established trades and services close their premises in the wake of the Internet buying revolution. New technological developments are changing consumers' needs as well as their shopping habits, and a whole new language is separating those who are ready to embrace the new world from those who are feeling bewildered by what is happening.

Of course, it is not the first time that society has been reshaped by technology. Earlier generations felt the impact of the Industrial Revolution, and our grandparents saw family-run shops, bespoke tailoring and other specialist services gradually replaced by the convenience of shopping in supermarkets, buying 'ready made' from department stores and catalogues. The difference now is the speed with which the current revolution is taking place.

Old business model	New business model
Service-led	Self-service
Quality costs more	Quality at discount
Brand loyalty	Superstar brands
Savings	Credit cards
Adult-led market	Youth market
Slow change	Fast change
Jobs for life	Multiple careers
In-house	Outsourcing
Employees	Associates
Valuing tradition	Embracing change
Analogue	Digital
Slow-paced	Fast-paced
Contact book	Social media
Word-of-mouth	Twitter

Never has change in the business world been so fast and as global as it is today, which means that never before has there been such scope to be a successful entrepreneur. We live in exciting times, times of immense opportunity. The business model has evolved; however, 'old' doesn't necessarily mean 'bad' and 'new' does not necessarily mean 'better ' or 'permanent'. Four important factors remain constant:

- PROFIT
- VALUE
- REPUTATION
- SERVICE

In a world in which an anonymous person can now pass judgement on your product or service online – influencing many other potential customers you have yet to meet – the 'old-fashioned' qualities of customer service, value for money and personal reputation are as important as they ever were. Understanding what people expect, what they want and what will lead them to decide to use or abuse your product or service is critical to the evaluation process and will contribute to your survival and success. Market research is vital; creating a customer profile is essential, as well as assessing the optimum price for your product or service.

HOW TO TURN A GOOD IDEA INTO SUCCESSFUL START-UP

If you are wondering whether your new business idea is a good one, or whether you will make money in the first year, there are several elements involved in initial project evaluation:

- Step into the business SWOT spot and assess the viability of the business.
- Take stock of your personal skills and the skills you may need to make your business work.

- DISCover your relationship with risk. Do you have what it takes to run with your idea?
- What could go wrong – how risky is this? Can you overcome the potential downside?
- Think 'sales'. Your sales and pricing strategy are the keys to a successful business plan. Consider how viable the business could be in one, three, five or ten years and beyond.
- Most important of all – ask yourself how much you care about your idea. Is it driving you to succeed? Is it enveloping you with enthusiasm and making you buzz with energy?

Ask yourself:

'Is my gut feeling telling me to Do It! or Ditch It?'

'On a scale of 1 to 10, how badly do I want to make it work?'

When you are at the *What?* stage of evaluating your business concept, anything is possible, but not everything is viable. Be careful not to make assumptions. If you need some experienced advice, seek out people who can help you gather the insight you need.

If you know you want to steam ahead, commit some time to doing further research and prepare a thorough business plan, complete with a financial and a marketing strategy.

THE BUSINESS SWOT SPOT

Doing a value check in the form of a SWOT analysis is a useful way to take stock of the Strengths and Weaknesses of your business idea, factor in the Opportunities that will increase your chances of success and the Threats to its success and survival.

A SWOT analysis can be a very fast track to a DO IT! OR DITCH IT decision. I call this the SWOT SPOT (see page 77). It can be used to evaluate anything: you, your business, your competitors; it can be small-scale or big-picture. If too much of your analysis lies in the Weaknesses and Threats quadrants, the decision to Ditch It is usually quite easy, unless the scope for profit is so high that it is worth investing in ways to convert those aspects into Strengths and Opportunities.

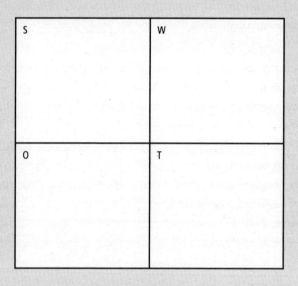

You can use the above template to do a quick SWOT of your own decision-making dilemma now. THE SWOT SPOT provides an immediate reality check that forces you to look at the immediate viability of your action, your idea or your business. It doesn't have to be in-depth to provide a useful litmus test for decision-making. Your own Strengths and Weaknesses are an important part of the mix.

The process works best as an ongoing cycle that is repeated again and again until each idea has been fully evaluated and you have formulated a solid plan. I use the approach so regularly within my businesses that I am barely aware that I am doing so. Many would-be entrepreneurs who are energised by new ideas will benefit from the rigour of this approach.

IT'S TIME FOR A PERSONAL CHECKUP

Just as wise travellers will ensure they have been inoculated against potentially fatal diseases before they leave home, so, too, it is important to make sure that you are not carrying anything with you that will let you down on your journey. That health test begins by evaluating your own skill set and experience.

For example, when setting up a business, ask yourself:

'What key skills do I have that will support me when running with my idea?'

'How much do I know about the business niche that I am focusing on?'

'What level of business management experience have I had to date?'

'Can I successfully lead a team?'

'What kinds of life experience will help me to run my businesses?'

'Can I afford to give up the day job?'

'How do I react under pressure?'

'How badly do I want this idea to work?'

'How much experience do I have of selling?'

Being weak in some areas is not necessarily a disadvantage because further knowledge will come, through learning and with experience. However, to give your good idea the best chance of start-up success, it is important to understand where your strengths lie and what skills you lack so that you can fill the gap in other ways and via other people. I talk elsewhere about the importance of investing in self-development. Being realistic about your skills and abilities is an important part of the evaluation stage.

'Building a business is not down to luck – it is a process, and a skill, that can be learned like any other.'

Building a business is not down to luck – it is a process, and a skill, that can be learned like any other. The future success of any enterprise depends on the ability of the entrepreneur to 'think like a business owner' and their ability to evaluate and manage risk.

Sell ability

In my opinion, the most important skill to have in business is an understanding of sales. You can be a master craftsman, a brilliant life coach, run a consultancy that provides exceptional advice – but if you can't get customers and clients through the door you will eventually fail. If you are not comfortable selling, then you will need to factor a salesperson into your annual budget. Without a sales person, your business is highly vulnerable, no matter how strong the business prospect might be.

At the end of the day, you need to decide who will sell. You can do it, you can recruit someone to do it, you outsource it; but Do It! Too many people lose business because they are too slow to follow up enquiries or sales leads.

*'Remember – another day older is
another day colder ...'*

Peter Thomson

DISCover YOUR RELATIONSHIP WITH RISK AND DECISION-MAKING

It is often said that entrepreneurs are risk takers, but having worked with many self-made millionaires I can safely say that the risks they take are *calculated* risks. They don't dive in without knowing or testing the depth of the water first. Your DISC personality profile will tell you a lot about your relationship with risk, and how you are likely to react under pressure. Each DISC personality style (see page 56) has a built-in safety valve that will determine the type and level of risk they are comfortable with. They will also develop strategies to neutralise or minimise that risk.

The DISC risk factor

D-styles. Welcome a challenge. They are 'comfortable feeling uncomfortable'. Being strong-willed and determined, they hate to lose or to lose face. If you are mainly D in style your attitude to risk is a very important factor to be aware of, as it could be your Achilles heel. Wanting to appear tough or invincible could lead D-styles to make fast or rash decisions without fully considering the ramifications. Knowing when to stop or when to ask for advice or further information may 'save the day' and safeguard the success of the business for High D-styles.

I-styles. Being impulsive, optimistic and enthusiastic means that I-styles may miss vital detail during the evaluation stage and therefore come unstuck after they have committed to taking action. I-styles may well say yes because they feel they can't say no, and then worry about how to deliver later. Being too trusting, over-optimistic and relying upon their instincts may lead them to work without a formal contract, which can be the death of a High-I business. Feeling that something is right is no replacement for the clarity and value of a business plan. A deal struck on a handshake is no substitute for a signed contract when things get rocky.

S-styles. Security is a strong driving force behind the S-style, so the thought of risk can leave them cold. S-styles are highly risk-averse. However, risk can also occur as a result of being over-cautious and delaying a necessary decision. Like the I-style, the S-style is a people person and can be overly trusting. Decision-making is a consultative process for an S-style person. S-styles are less likely to take big risks and will want to put in place safeguards to minimise any chance of danger; however, they may not be their own best representative when negotiating terms.

C-styles. Being risk-adverse and with a gift for foreseeing all eventualities, the C-styles are unlikely to be caught unawares. C-styles are methodical, cautious and will research and recheck before making big decisions. However, the C-style can suffer from paralysis of analysis because they are forever waiting for everything to be perfect before moving forward, always wanting just a bit more detail. Their comfort zone (see page 22) lies in business planning. In extreme, the C-style may have several excellent business ideas, but get so caught up in planning that they never fire the starting gun.

> Founder of Diva Cosmetics Emma Wimhurst (who is a combination of D-, I- and C-styles) remembers how she felt the day she walked into her first top-level business meeting in New Look to pitch her first range of own-brand products. 'I was so nervous, that I had over-prepared for the meeting and had created enough samples for an entire cosmetic range. I can still remember how disappointed I was when I received my first order for only several thousand nail polishes. I was so far out of my comfort zone that it took me a while to realise what a successful outcome that order was! After that I felt invincible. I never went into a meeting as worried or as nervous again.'

Being aware of your relationship with risk is useful because it may impact on your decision to do or ditch your business idea. If you tend towards the S- or C-style, then you can choose to 'try on' the D- or the I-style to consider your options from a different point of view, or vice versa.

If your usual preference is to stay within your comfort zone, you may miss opportunities for growth and development. Instead, you can consciously imagine how it would feel to step out of your comfort zone and adopt the outlook of the other styles. Stretch your comfort zone by weighing up your choices from all angles before you drive ahead or abandon your business idea.

For example, when a High C-style person has to attend a networking event, it can be a nerve-wracking experience for them. However, it will be possible consciously to raise their I-traits, to become more outgoing, and their S-traits, to focus on other people, for the short period of time they are there.

Decision-making tools:

'Trying on' your business idea means entering the stretch zone (page 22). This works very well in partnership with taking a mental stroll along the DISCovery walk (page 144). Are you comfortable feeling uncomfortable? Have you considered your idea from every angle?

UNDERSTANDING NEEDS vs. WANTS

Every successful business idea fulfils a *need*, a *want*, or solves a problem – and needs to do it in a way that stands out alongside the competition.

Stack it high, sell it cheap

When under pressure, many businesses will try to compete by lowering prices. For example, in a major inner-city area that I know well, there are a number of health clubs. Initially there were two clubs based across the road from one other, each charging £42 per month for membership. During a financial downturn, club membership in the fitness sector began to diminish.

- Club A decided to rebrand and reduce its prices to £15 per month. It used this as a hook to gain mass numbers by taking a 'stack it high, sell it cheap' approach.
- Club B lowered its price to £25 per month but made no significant changes to its service.
- A new club, Club C, has now opened up on the block, which is charging only £10 per month. All three businesses are within a five-minute walk of each other.

The trouble is, if you compete only on price, you are on a fast and slippery downward slope to cash-flow disaster. Like health and fitness books and DVDs, membership sales are as much about selling an intention and an aspiration as helping to deliver a result. A major price reduction means that twice as many members are then needed because they are only paying half the price. There are several danger points in this approach:

- More people (because they are paying less money) will create more usage which means more wear and tear on equipment.
- If customers buy on price alone they will probably not be loyal customers. When a competitor presents a cheaper option they will probably leave.
- If you change your membership fees you also change your customer profile. Your new customers may drive away your existing customers, so make a conscious decision who you want to do business with.
- There may not be twice as many new customers in your area.

'Bear in mind that it can cost up to six times more to find a new customer than to keep an existing one.'

If you change the price you need to change other elements of your business, too. It is difficult to drop your price and maintain the same staffing levels or service. With this model, you will be aiming for the cheaper end and the mass market. For example, Club C has no staff, preferring a turnstile-entry system, no sauna, steam room spa and a primarily self-service product. If, on the other hand, you are aiming at the top end or the luxury market, the quality of your product, the level of service and your price point need to be correspondingly high.

The problem comes when one area of the business model is not in line with the other. In the health club model above, Club B is particularly vulnerable, because its price point is neither low enough to compete with the cheap end of the market nor perceived as high enough value to appeal to the top end of the market. It has inadvertently lost its USP (unique selling point) because it is are no longer exclusive, and is not the cheapest either.

At the other end of the spectrum is a company like Harrods, which is synonymous with luxury and where tourists are known to buy any item they can afford in order to receive a carrier bag bearing the Harrods logo.

THE VIEW FROM THE TOP

Not long ago I visited Harrods to look, out of curiosity, for one of the most expensive perfumes in the world. For those who don't know, it is not Chanel; it is not Yves Saint Laurent; it is a perfume with the unassuming name of Clive Christian. It is a firm with a long and established history that has always remained focused on the discerning end of the luxury market. The most expensive bottle of Clive Christian currently costs £115,000 and it has a five-carat diamond on the top of the bottle. Now no one can possibly *need* a bottle of perfume costing that amount of money

– but apparently a select range of customers from around the world do *want* it enough to spend that amount of money.

The more luxurious the item, the greater the sales experience has to be. When I spoke to Marcel Van Der Merwe, the assistant manager in Harrods' Roja Dove Haute Parfumerie, he had a fascinating story to tell about every perfume on the shelf. He made the brands come alive to the extent that he was almost taking you on a journey with him. It was wonderful. He has the gift of making every customer he speaks to feel as if they want *and* need to become a part of the perfume story.

He also had great customer intelligence, and knew that the majority of his customers lived within a two-mile radius of the store. It was clear that he understood not only his products, but also his customers. Part of the evaluation process for a business idea is always to test the market to ensure that the needs and wants of your clients and customers are met. He understood my need to understand, too, and arranged for me to meet the founder of the parfumerie, Roja Dove.

Roja Dove has a passion for excellence. He is world renowned as the 'maestro of fragrance' and he owns Harrods' Roja Dove Haute Parfumerie. I asked him how his business had been doing during the recession. His answer interested me: during the first year their turnover was 20 per cent up on the previous year; during the second year it was 40 per cent up.

The perfume industry is a billion-dollar industry, but Roja does not try to compete by lowering his prices. He is proud to stock the world's most expensive perfumes. Like me, he dislikes hearing a sales assistant use phrases such as, 'This is the most popular ...', 'This is our best seller ...' and so on. That kind of language doesn't make the product or service sound special.

Roja is passionate about people and he invests heavily in training his parfumerie team. Far from adopting the usual 'spray and pray technique' (his words) that are adopted by many stores, Roja is determined that his team should have both industry and product knowledge. His highly personal approach to selling has the ability to turn a commercial commodity into something precious and desirable, while delivering an exceptional customer experience.

He knows that no one needs to spend £115,000 on perfume but his approach proves that if you produce what people want, and can sell it in an environment and in a style that customers appreciate and identify with, then no price limit can be set on its value.

The lesson to be learned from the success of Harrods and Roja Dove is that, whatever you feel your product or service is worth, you need to operate in an environment in which the minimum price is in accordance with your pricing. If you are shopping somewhere that sells high-priced goods, it alters the customer's perspective of what is expensive. Clive Christian would not sell at a high price on a street market – even if the market was in the most exclusive street in the world.

When selling pizza by the slice at a roadside stall you will charge by the slice; when you sell pizza in an Italian bistro you will charge for the whole pizza. The pizza could be exactly the same, but the 'want' for customers at the street stall will be speed of service and a cheap price. The 'want' for the diners in the restaurant will be quality of food and service with no sense of being rushed.

All too often when the number of customers is small, new business owners feel tempted to lower their prices; but that just makes your job of selling more difficult. Lowering your prices won't necessarily encourage more people through your door. The answer is to make sure that you are selling alongside other retail outlets, goods and services that are targeting similar customers and in the right price bracket.

TESTING THE MARKET

Asking yourself key questions about the market for your product or service before you launch it is essential. Asking potential customers the same questions, and assessing what the competition is doing, is even better – because it will help to build a clearer picture and help you to avoid making expensive assumptions in your business plan. Ask yourself and others:

> *'Who will buy your product or service?'*
> *'At what price will they buy it?'*
> *'How will they buy it (online, in-store, mail order etc)?'*
> *'How often will they buy it?'*
> *'Who else can they buy it from?'*
> *'Where can they get it cheaper?'*
> *'What else will they buy?'*

A common mistake is to over-estimate the number of clients, projects or footfall that you will experience in the first year of trading, or to invest in premises before you really need them. Testing the market before you begin will help you to make adjustments along the way. Many a successful start-up has begun at home; many retailers have started out on the Internet or with a market stall, to avoid overheads. A useful strategy is always to start (very) small and grow gradually.

- *What is the average spend that you will need per customer?*
- *What is the average daily footfall in your location?*
- *Do the potential customers match your customer profile?*
- *How much turnover do you need per day/week/month to break even?*

Figuring out how many customers you will need, on a daily, weekly, monthly basis to meet your targets and make your business profitable, will help you to stay on track and keep your costs under control (see also Step 6: HOW MUCH?).

THINK 'SALES' AT ALL TIMES

Not every idea is commercially driven and not every business decision will be made solely with the financial return in mind. However, I find it incredibly sad and frustrating when anyone who has invested time, energy and focus in setting up a business has to return to employment on a full- or part-time basis because of cash-flow problems.

Businesses fail not because people aren't good enough at what they do, but because they aren't effective at generating new or repeat business – or, worse, they don't manage their accounts or time and under-charge for their goods or services. Too many people set up their business believing 'When I am ready, they will come'. That is far from the reality of what will happen. You will need to tell as many people as possible that you exist and to keep communicating that message as clearly as you can – again and again and again – via as many media as possible (see Step 5: HOW? for ideas about routes to market).

> *'Too many people set up their business believing "When I am ready, they will come". That is far from the reality of what will happen.'*

Start with the end in mind. Ask yourself – what is your customer profile? Know your market and position yourself as an expert. Being a successful businessperson is not only about being professionally excellent, it is about 'nailing your niche' and running your business efficiently: prospecting for clients, managing costs and marketing *yourself* or your business in an ongoing and cost-effective way.

'Remember: A generalist seeks clients, but a client seeks a specialist.'

As a specialist, it will be easier for other people to find you or to recommend you to other people. Very often you can charge more for your time because there are fewer competitors offering your service.

Ask yourself:

'How much do I need to earn per year?' (and how does that break down?).

'What are my running costs?' (premises, bills, rent, living costs and so on).

'How many clients do I need to make this work – per year, per month, per week?' (people often don't know this).

'How much do I need to allow for tax and National Insurance?' (consider setting up a separate bank account to put the money aside).

'What is the market rate, and what is my scale of charges?' (do some market research).

'Have I taken account of seasonal variations?' (for example, December is likely to be slow in some businesses and a peak time in others).

'Is this more or less than the number of clients I want?' (alter pricing accordingly).

'How am I going to find them?' (target your marketing).

The starting point is always a business plan. It doesn't need to be elaborate, but it needs to be very clear. Check that your price point is aligned with your level of service and the quality of your product. If you are focusing on mass-market sales of low-price items, you will need to keep your customer service polite but fast-moving. If you are selling a specialist service to a niche market, you will need to provide excellent client care. A specialist business has fewer customers than a mass-market business – but the ones you have will want to feel cared for and remembered. It is vital for repeat business. Whatever your business model, it is important to know what differentiates you from your competitors.

Your USP will get you noticed. It will set you apart and ensure you are remembered. If you create something so essential or desirable that everyone *wants* it – they will find a reason to *need* it, too.

THE ADVANCE OF THE 5–9

Many people who are setting up in business are still employees. They return home after a 9–5 day and work long into the night on their new venture. They are known as the 5–9ers and they are a growing group of entrepreneurs. Although this kind of lifestyle is unsustainable in the long term, in the short term it may be very wise. A budding entrepreneur may want to become self-employed full-time, but knows that they need to take the low-risk approach in the short term. What they ideally want and what they need may not yet be aligned. So 'don't give up the day job' is sound advice until you have tested the market sufficiently to know that you can afford to commit to your business full-time.

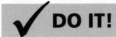 **DO IT!**

TOP TEN TIPS FOR EVALUATING YOUR BUSINESS IDEA

- **Develop a customer profile.** Identify who you want to attract through your door.
- **Nail your market niche.** Decide what you want to be known for – and market your business accordingly.
- **Know your worth.** Work out your pricing point – and develop a range of services and scale of charges that reflects what is realistic.
- **Be customer-focused.** Avoid using jargon and always use language your clients will relate to.
- **Be the best.** Make sure you are the best in your field so that people will recommend you.
- **Know the competition.** Analyse your competitors and make sure that you are competitively priced and better than them in some way – but don't become preoccupied with them; focus on your own business.
- **Decide to get noticed.** Your website is your shop window. Make sure that it looks professional and reflects the quality of your service.
- **Analyse your business.** Develop a business plan, a marketing strategy and a budget – and use them to analyse your business every day.
- **Take control.** Set up a system to keep a track of your cash flow. It is much easier to do this before you launch your business. But don't let a spreadsheet rule your thinking. Remember: you are running your business, not reacting to it.
- **Get professional advice from day one.** Don't struggle unassisted. There is a wealth of advice available on your doorstep. Get a business mentor, join a business network and consult your accountant.

DO IT! OR DITCH IT CHECKLIST

WHAT?

Evaluating the concept

When you think about launching your business idea, how confident are you that the idea is commercially viable? Are you feeling ready to drive ahead or anxious about the thought of what you may have taken on? Your feelings signpost your true level of belief and help you to assess what you want or need to make your ultimate decision to Do It! or Ditch It.

Use the checklist below to assess your current state of mind on a scale of 1 to 10 to see whether you are ready to get started. Consider each characteristic and mark where on the line your state of mind lies. Do you feel like Ditching? Or are you ready to Do?

This exercise does not evaluate the idea or the decision itself. There are no 'good feelings' or 'bad feelings' and no rights or wrongs. It is a way to evaluate your frame of mind.

On balance, are you in a 'Do It!' frame of mind? Or is that critical voice inside your head suggesting you should 'Ditch It' and look more closely at the path you have chosen? Only those projects that we feel passionate about are likely ultimately to succeed.

CHECK YOUR MINDSET

On a scale of 1 to 10, how close are you to your goal?

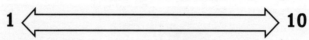

1   **10**

The 'Ditch It' Warning Signs	The 'Do It!' Mindset
I am unsure of the market research	I have confidence in our market
I can't make the numbers work	The numbers are realistic
I am putting things off	I am determined to launch
I am worried	I feel positive
I can see only obstacles	I can see several solutions
I have no contacts	I can network well
I have serious doubts	I trust my judgement
I am preoccupied with the competition	We have a clear point of difference
I am past caring	I really want this to work
I need to know more	I am ready to act

WHAT ACTIONS WILL TAKE YOU ONE STEP CLOSER TO YOUR GOAL?

WRITE THEM HERE

STEP 2: WHY?

Why is your idea important to you?

PERSONAL MOTIVATION

*'If you know "why" you want to take action
you'll work out "how" to achieve it.'*

Step 2: WHY? focuses on personal motivation. It will help you to recognise why some ideas fire your enthusiasm, while others leave you cold. The choices you make each day to either DO or DITCH an idea, a behaviour or a decision will eventually add up to become the whole of your life. Knowing 'why' you feel motivated to take action will help you to build a business that you will want to succeed, resulting in positive outcomes.

Beware the danger zone: if you find yourself wasting time or procrastinating over daily tasks, the chances are you have lost your motivation or your point of focus. The Do It! or Ditch It approach will help to remind you why your idea is important and what you want to achieve.

It is an interesting fact that most people spend proportionally longer planning a two-week holiday than they do the other fifty weeks of the working year. Why is that? It is because they are completely focused on the goal, they have a passion for the task and are fully engaged in delivering the best possible result – within a fixed time frame.

The most important part of goal setting is always the WHY. It is your motivation. When the going gets tough, the *why* keeps us on track. People who have lost focus and direction have often lost sight of why they are doing the task – or what their motivation was for beginning it in the first place. In the words of Brian Tracy, 'You can't hit a target you can't see.'

When we arrive at our holiday destination we know that time is of the essence and we don't want to waste it. Some people will go to the extent of preparing a detailed schedule of the whole two weeks, listing places to visit and things to do – ticking them off the list as the days progress – but it would never occur to them to apply the same rigorous approach to their daily workload.

Goal setting alone is not enough. We need to strengthen personal behaviours that will support our goals. Ask yourself:

> 'What new behaviours do you need to 'DO' each and every day that will take you closer to your goal?'
> 'What behaviours do you need to 'DITCH' that could sabotage your goal?'

I have worked with a number of Olympic athletes over the past few years and it is easy to see why they have achieved incredible success. They don't just know *how* to compete in a certain sport, they know *why* they compete. Their focus is fixed firmly upon the Olympic goal. Their behaviour is consistently aligned with attaining that primary goal. Everything else is secondary. Professional athletes train themselves to hone the qualities, attitudes, characteristics and behaviours that will contribute to their success. There is no room for a negative thought, an 'off day', a moan, a groan or a wasted second.

I see very similar characteristics in successful entrepreneurs. They, too, consistently display determination, discipline, focus, drive, passion. They have the ability to perform under pressure, they are competitive, have self-belief and the ability to bounce back after setbacks. Many commit to excellence and always look to exceed their personal best. Many would confess to neglecting other aspects of their life – socialising, holidays, home-building, having children because their business goal is their priority.

> **'The greater danger for most of us is not that our aim is too high and we miss it, but that it is too low and we hit it.'**
>
> *Michelangelo*

Usain Bolt is the current world and Olympic record holder for the 100 metres. He won a gold medal in 9.58 seconds at the World Championships in Berlin in 2009. The question is, how long did it take him to be able to run 100 metres in less than ten seconds? It would have taken years of training, discipline, practice and repetition. The same often applies to actors. It can take years of hard graft for them to become an overnight success. George Clooney had been working professionally for sixteen years before he found 'instant' recognition. Many spend years treading the boards in repertory theatre before getting their West End break.

If you find yourself constantly distracted from the task at hand, ask yourself what you are focusing on instead. What is your true primary goal? As Aristotle said, 'We are what we repeatedly do.' The important thing is to know what you want, why you want it and to make sure that every day your actions and behaviours take you closer to your true objective.

It may seem an obvious thing to say, but knowing *why* your idea is important to you and *why* it drives you forward is key to your success. Those who feel passionate about their ideas and know why they want to take action are more animated, focused and persuasive than those who don't. They can make things happen more readily and encourage others to buy into what they are aiming to achieve. They will also find it easier to stay focused on the goal without distraction – for the duration of the plan.

Many ideas are commercially viable. Whether or not they turn out to be successful depends on your passion for the concept, your belief in yourself and the steps you put in place to plan your business journey in advance. Think of a problem, a need or a want; find a way to fulfil it and you have the kernel of an idea for a sound business. But only consider developing the idea further if you feel consumed by enthusiasm. Remind yourself that if you don't know why you are doing something or feel no driving commitment to making things work, then it will be harder to stay on track when things become challenging. It can be a tough lesson to learn.

I have been asked to get involved with setting up many excellent business opportunities over the years, but I know that I could only remain involved if the whole concept fired me with enthusiasm. There is little point in buying a tool-hire franchise if the thought of doing DIY leaves you cold; or opening a florist's if you are allergic to pollen. You can, of course, but it is not a path that I would recommend unless the opportunity is too good to miss and you can engage others to run it long term.

Multimillionaire and serial entrepreneur James Caan agrees. As CEO of private equity firm Hamilton Bradshaw, he is approached daily by entrepreneurs who are seeking investment for their business venture. He has invested over £2 million to date as an investment dragon on BBC TV's *Dragons' Den*. For James, understanding the true motivation of the person who wants him to invest is vital, and can be the deciding factor when listening to a business pitch. He told me:

'If someone says "I'm passionate", "I'm driven", "I'm motivated", I will say, "That's great ... the question is why?" "Why are you passionate, why are you driven, why are you doing this and why is it important to you?" What I am really asking is "What are you going to do to make this successful; are you going to be there at seven in the morning; are you going to be the last to leave; are you prepared to work weekends? What are you really prepared to do?"'

For James, success is all about having a reason to be driven, a reason to be motivated. He continues:

'If your only reason to be in business is to make a lot of money, that means nothing. Anyone can say that. Even the wish for a nicer car or a better lifestyle lacks substance. When I am trying to decide whether someone is worth backing, I need to be able to identify with the reason they want to be successful; what that success is all about. Identifying the passion and the motive is always the trigger for me. That won't be in the PowerPoint slides and it may not be in the presentation, but it does make all the difference as to whether I select someone or not.'

 DO IT!

- Taking a DISC self-assessment questionnaire (see page 56) will act like a mirror that shows you what motivates you in your work and what holds you back.
- The DISC 'drive' below will help you to assess how you decide 'why' your idea is important and whether you are ready to Do It! or Ditch It.

WEALTH IS NOT AN AMOUNT OF MONEY – IT IS A STATE OF MIND

As a businessperson, you may think you are motivated solely by a desire to be wealthy, but that is very rarely the case. The majority of business owners need to care about what they do to make that money. They are motivated as much by the sense of personal satisfaction that comes from making things happen and a job well done as they are by the financial rewards. That is why so many businesspeople find it hard to stop working and relax, even on holiday; and why many others want to make sure that those around them also enjoy the material benefits of success.

Many of the millionaires I have worked with were driven initially either by a desire no longer to be poor, or by a straightforward wish to build a successful business. In many ways, becoming a millionaire (or a billionaire – there are more and more of them about these days) is a by-product of success, rather than the main goal.

Successful property tycoon Gill Fielding explains: 'I always knew I wanted to be wealthy, so I have always been driven to succeed and make a difference for myself.' But, equally, she will admit that in the early days of her career she had no game plan; she simply focused on one deal at a time. More recently, as a subject of the Channel 4 programme *The Secret Millionaire*, she realised that she was no longer afraid of being poor, because she trusts her business instincts. Incidentally, Gill gave away £250,000 on the show, and remains one of the highest donors to have taken part in the programme.

> 'During the filming of *The Secret Millionaire*, I found myself living incognito and literally back where I started in the East End, instinctively stashing away £2 of my daily £10 allowance in a sock, in case of need. As well as the immense pleasure it gave me to help others during the course of that programme, the experience made me realise is that I will always be a millionaire – because even if I lost it all, I would still be saving and strategising. I know that I have an instinct for making money and over the years I have identified a formula for success. Everyone in business has that potential; they just need to understand how it can be done.'

Much has been written about the characteristics of millionaires. My own observations are simple:

- They believe in themselves.
- They are driven to succeed.
- They are focused.
- They like to be in control.
- They love what they do and they have an enthusiasm for their work.
- They tend to be extremely competitive and want to win.
- The blaze a trail rather than follow others.
- They listen to good advice – but then they make their own decisions.
- They take responsibility for their actions.
- They recognise what they need to give up in order to gain.
- They are driven by a passion to fulfil their own dream – not someone else's.
- They accept success or failure – and move on.
- They live below their means.

Millionaire motivation usually comes from a positive place that drives the business owner forwards towards their goal. It is an active rather than a reactive response. Rather than becoming preoccupied with what their competitors are up to, they have their own plan to become the most successful in the marketplace. Successful businesspeople know why they are in business and will make things happen. They very rarely look back and have regrets.

The DISC guide to personal drive has been created as an immediate test for your own level of motivation. 'The DISC drive' will help you to be alert to aspects of your personality that may hold you back. (Revisit Chapter 3 for a reminder of the principles of DISC – and remember that most people are a mix of more than one dominant trait.)

DISCover YOUR PERSONAL MOTIVATION

It can be helpful to reflect on your core motives for being in business. Knowing *why* you want something will enable you to develop a laser-like focus and an unshakeable belief that you can make things happen. Understanding the *why* will drive you to see *how* you can achieve your goals. The Do It! or Ditch It DISC -drive will help you to ensure that your potential idea is aligned with your values and that you have the drive and determination to make it work.

The primary question for everyone, whether D, I, S, or C is:

'Why do I feel motivated by this idea?'

D-style

D-styles are the most competitive group. If they are in business to make a profit, they will have little trouble in deciding to exclude ideas that waste time and resources, or that don't fit the long-term goal.

If you are a D-style, you will need to acknowledge at some point that attention to detail may be required and you may need to slow down (as frustrating as that may feel!). You may need to outsource the collation of facts or figures, the dotting of the i's and the crossing of the t's, to those in your team who have a C-style profile.

> The D-style motto is often: *'Ready – FIRE – Aim'*

Typical responses from a D-style may be:

'I can make it happen.'
'It will be a challenge and I will enjoy raising my game.'
'I can get fast results.'
'I am competitive.'

'Judge me by my results, not by my methods.'

The danger point is: *'I will worry about the detail later. I just want to get started.'*

The DISC drive is: *'On a scale of one to ten, how much do I want this?'*

The decision-making strategy is:
Employ someone with some C in their profile or acknowledge the need to step up yourself in this regard. Think through the process and the detail before you decide to run with your idea.

I-style

I-styles will often have trouble settling on a single idea. The concept of a portfolio career was made for this group of people. They find it easy to start things, and much harder to see them through, because they become distracted by the next bright, shiny idea and the gleam of its potential.

If you are an I-style, you may need to acknowledge that you can be over- optimistic. You will need to take a long, hard look at the downside (however painful that may be). Like the D-style, you will need to slow down and get all the facts (or get someone to do this for you) before you proceed.

> **The I-style motto is often: *'Ready – Aim – TALK'***

Typical responses from an I-style may be:
'I will make it fun.'
'I will persuade.'
'I will be enthusiastic and positive.'
'I will gain recognition and others will like me.'

'I will network, meet interesting people and be sociable.'
'I will enjoy learning new skills.'
'I will look for new opportunities.'

The danger point is: *'Talking can feel like doing – without the results.'*

The DISC drive is: *'On a scale of one to ten, what are you prepared to do to achieve the goal?'*

The decision-making strategy is:
Get properly focused on your end goal and how you are going to get there. Don't just talk: take action and see it through.

S-style

S-styles like to take things in turn and complete one task at a time when allowed. The S-styles like to see things through to completion. They are great listeners and team players and are often found in customer support/service roles.

If you are an S-style, you may need to acknowledge that acceptance of change may be an issue. Just because you have a plan in place does not mean that it can't change as you progress. Sometimes you have to adapt and modify to succeed.

> The S motto is often: **'Ready – aim – DELAY'** (because I'm not sure)

Typical responses from an S-style may be:
'What element of risk is involved?'
'If it ain't broke, don't fix it.'
'Will everyone be OK with this?'
'I can see how others will benefit.'
'The supply chain will be all-important.'

The danger points are: *'I'm not sure about this, the outcome is not certain.'*
'I may delay important decisions if I think they will have a negative impact on others.'

The DISC drive is: *'On a scale of one to ten, how much do I trust that this is a fail-safe idea?'*

The decision-making strategy is:
Take the time to research the pros and cons. Find out how the decision may be of benefit to all.

C-style

C-styles are often perfectionists, which means that their ideas may get bogged down in detail. The need to 'have all your ducks in a row' and get everything right before getting started may mean that ideas lose their momentum, or that they miss the moment, because a competitor brings the same idea to the marketplace more quickly.

> **The C-style motto is often: *'Ready, aim; Ready, aim; Ready, aim ...'***

Typical responses from a C-style may be:
'What is the process?'
'What is the timescale?'
'What EXACTLY must be done?'
'What could go wrong?'
'I could make an excellent job of that.'
'The facts stack up.'
'Is it fail-safe?'
'I need more information.'

The danger point is: *'Paralysis of analysis.'*

The DISC drive is: *'On a scale of one to ten, how ready am I to START?'*

The decision-making strategy is:
Believe that you have enough information to get started and that your eye for detail won't let you down in the longer term. Acknowledge the fact that you may need to be more outgoing and relational in order to achieve your objective.

The Do It! or Ditch It DISC-drive:
- If your DISC-drive answers are close to ten, then DO IT!
- If your answers are closer to five or below, then it may be better to take another look, or DITCH IT and turn your attention elsewhere.

WILL vs. SHOULD

I interview hundreds of business owners each year for the Entrepreneurs' Business Academy. It is one of the aspects of the work that I love the most, because everyone's business journey is different and people light up when they talk about something they care about.

Sometimes, however, it becomes clear that the business owner is not living their own dream, that they are trying to fulfil someone else's expectations. That always worries me. Personal development expert Anthony Robbins employs a memorable phrase: he talks about people 'should-ing' all over themselves. When I hear people using the 'should' word frequently, it is a warning sign and I will always delve deeper to find out more about what or who is behind their business dream.

Listen to yourself speak next time you are describing your

business idea or your activities to date. How often do you use the word 'should'?

'Should-ing' may denote several things:

- *Low personal motivation* – your heart is not really in it or you have a lack of belief.
- *Poor management skills* – your workload has become overwhelming and you fail to prioritise.
- *A sense of duty and obligation* – rather than drive and ambition, you are doing things for others rather than yourself or your project.

'Should-ing' is about looking backwards, not forwards. 'Should' leaves business owners stuck in what didn't happen rather than motivated by what 'will' happen. It is usually related to a lack of forward planning.

'Will-ing', on the other hand, suggests a positive mindset and a drive and willingness to propel things forwards. Turning 'should-ing' into 'will-ing' can have a dynamic impact on business development and personal motivation.

'I should have prepared better for the client meeting' becomes 'I will allocate diary time to plan ahead for the next meeting.'

'I shouldn't have missed the deadline' becomes 'I will plan more realistically. I will recruit some assistance.'

There is no place for 'should-ing' in the mind of a motivated business leader. With business ownership comes personal responsibility and a need for resilient leadership. Making appropriate decisions and sticking to them is important. Being clear about your goals, understanding your own motivation and behaving in a way that is consistent and congruent with achieving those goals will lead you towards success. 'Will-ing' rather than 'should-ing' is the only way forward.

'As Anthony Robbins always says, "Stop 'Should-ing' all over yourself."'

 **DO IT!**

TEN THINGS THAT WILL IMPROVE YOUR MOTIVATION

Whatever led you to your business idea, your chances of success will increase many times over if you have genuine belief in your idea and a passion for your business plan.

1. **Know 'why' you want to build your business.** If you are doing it just for the money you may struggle to stay motivated should you need to make personal sacrifices in terms of time and money, especially during the initial stages of the business.

2. **Self-belief.** Belief is what keeps you going when others knock you back; it's what helps keep you going when you are tired; it's what helps you to overcome unexpected obstacles and to see challenges as surmountable rather than a reason to quit.

3. **Be an expert.** Knowing your business will increase your confidence. Don't be tempted to set up a business in an area you know nothing about. Refurbishing your own home doesn't necessarily give you all the skills to be a property developer. If you're thinking of setting up a restaurant, eating in one isn't a prerequisite for owning one: unless, of course, you are partnering with someone with the necessary experience, or you are investing in the business and not necessarily working in it.

4. **Know what makes you different.** Having a USP that distinguishes you from your competitors will help you to sell your concept and help others to understand what you are offering and why they need it.

5. **'Get real'.** About your strengths and weaknesses so that you plan, prepare and put things right before you get started. Knowing where your weak spots lie and seeking professional expertise, or recruiting team members with those abilities, to balance your skills, can put you in a position of strength.

6. **Seek the company of others who want to succeed.** Not everyone has a 'can-do' attitude and, depending on what motivates you (see the DISC chapter on page 44), you may be too easily discouraged by those who are negative about you or your chances of success. Family and friends may not be the best choice if you are looking for a dispassionate view (unless they have the required knowledge), as they may feel protective of you or not want to change the status quo.

7. **Plan ahead:** Having a strong belief that something can work is *not the same* as blind optimism or letting your heart rule your head. Pour your belief into the practical structure of a business plan, stating your objectives, your financial plan and including a strategy and a time frame for achieving your goals.

8. **Embrace the passion.** It's not enough to *know* the business; you need to *love* it.

9. **Don't expect it to be easy.** Most new ventures take more time and money to get them off the ground than initially anticipated.

10. **Don't 'should'; always 'will'.** Valuable lessons can be learned from past mistakes, but getting stuck in regrets about what should have been will hold you back. Ditch the 'shoulds'; ask yourself 'why' you will succeed – and get ready to Do It!

Identify who can help you and who you may need to avoid

People are more willing to help each other to achieve their goals than you may imagine. If you know someone who has the skills to help you, approach them and ask them for their advice. Find a mentor who can help you in an objective way and will short-cut your route to success. A good piece of advice is 'Don't take advice from people less successful than yourself'.

Identifying who you need to avoid can be one of the trickier ones. Are there people close to you who undermine your ambitions; who are happy for you to stay the way you are because a change would threaten their status quo? At the end of the day, the only person who knows what is right for you is you. Others will catch up with you eventually if they care about you. Be brave, follow your dreams and start living today as if they are already a reality.

'Be brave, follow your dreams and start living today as if they are already a reality.'

DO IT! OR DITCH IT CHECKLIST

WHY?

Personal motivation

When you think about developing your current project, what is your state of mind? Are you feeling motivated to drive ahead or overwhelmed by the thought of what you may have taken on? When deciding whether to forge ahead with an idea it can be helpful to take stock and consider how you are feeling about it. Your feelings signpost your true level of motivation and help you to assess what you want or need to make your ultimate decision.

Try using the simple scale that follows to assess your current state of mind to see whether you are ready to get started. Consider each characteristic below and rate each on a scale of 1 to 10.

This exercise does not evaluate the idea or the decision itself. There are no 'good feelings' or 'bad feelings' and no rights or wrongs. It is a way to evaluate your frame of mind, and it will show you whether your inner doubter or inner cheerleader is shouting the loudest.

On balance, are you in a 'Do It!' frame of mind? Or is that critical voice inside your head suggesting you should 'Ditch it' and look more closely at the path you have chosen? Only those projects that we feel passionate about are likely ultimately to succeed.

CHECK YOUR MINDSET

On a scale of 1 to 10, how close are you to your goal?

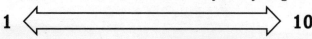

1   **10**

The 'Ditch It' Warning Signs	The 'Do It!' Mindset
Can't do	Can do
Don't care	Care passionately
Tired	Energised
Procrastination	Determined action
I know all I need to know	I have so much more to learn from others
Rigid	Adaptable
Only sees obstacles	Seeks solutions
Doubts ability	Trusts ability
I should	I will
Dwells on past mistakes	Looks to the future

WHAT ACTIONS WILL TAKE YOU ONE STEP CLOSER TO YOUR GOAL?

WRITE THEM HERE

STEP 3: WHERE?

Where are you heading?

PLANNING

'We judge ourselves by our intentions.
Others judge us by our actions.'

The Disney Institute

Step 3: WHERE? focuses on the importance of planning and prioritising, and how to use your time wisely to implement those plans. It is important to look before you leap. Have you decided on the short-, mid- and long-term goals for your business? *Do* make business planning a daily management habit. *Ditch* terminal drift.

Beware the danger zone: for some, planning is a comfort zone. They will happily plan until the cows come home. Their pattern is 'Ready, aim; Ready, aim ...' It makes them feel that they are getting somewhere – but they never fire the gun. At the other extreme are those who rush ahead with no plan at all, and suddenly find themselves in hot water. Their pattern is 'Ready, FIRE... Aim'. The Do It! or Ditch It approach increases your awareness of your decision-making style, so you can be sure to get ready, take aim and then fire – on all cylinders and in the ideal order of action.

Every journey begins with a destination and a route map. In business, your route map is your business plan. If you are entering new territory you will need to be prepared. A good idea will only become a profitable venture when there is a plan of action, and when that action plan is implemented.

Your business plan provides a snapshot of your intentions and helps you stay on track. Entire books have been written on the importance of business plans and how to put one together. Some of my favourites are included in Further Resources, at the end of the book. This chapter looks at how we make the big picture decisions concerning business structure long-term strategy. It also looks at the everyday decisions: how we prioritise tasks and get the job done.

Decisions are made at every moment of every day, whether or not we make them consciously – even *not* making a decision is a decision!

THE POWER OF PERSONAL FOCUS

The success of every business depends upon the laser-like focus and personal drive of the business owner. This attitude is encapsulated for me by the approach of Matt Dyer, now a millionaire, who I first met when he was 16 years old:

MATT DYER'S STORY

When I was 12 I set myself a goal to become a millionaire by the age of 30. I didn't know how I was going to achieve it, but I had complete belief that 'if you work hard, you're good at what you do, and you always deliver what you say you are going to deliver, then good things will happen for you'. So in my early teens, when my friends were out socialising, I devoted myself instead to learning as much about business as possible and taking action towards making my million. I felt driven towards achieving my goal.

My first 'real' job when I was 16 was working for Bev James and her husband, Dave. They ran a chain of health clubs at the time and they taught me everything there was to know about the industry. I worked for them as a gym instructor and an aerobics instructor and gained invaluable skills in sales and presentation that I still use today. However, my opportunity for success came later. I had set up a training organisation called ITC Learning and Development Limited. In 2004, the Financial Services Authority (FSA) became responsible for regulating the insurance industry and so I set myself the task of training the 27,000 people who needed to learn to understand compliance issues before the legislation went live in 2005. I worked flat out for eighteen months to complete the task; and that was how I made my first million – in my 30th year.

The industry I am in is ruled by very strict legal requirements, so my decisions need to be validated against legal requirements, but in general I would say that I am quite instinctive in my decision-making. My approach is based very much on my own judgement, backed up by detail. I am confident in my own abilities and I have the courage of my convictions. Although I do listen to my colleague, ultimately the decision-making process rests with me. If I am certain about something then I will go with it; if I am not, I will make sure that I am certain about it before I go for it.

These days I believe that it is important to have multiple goals in business and to be true to yourself in what you do. One goal is dangerous, because if you don't achieve it you will tend to look back and consider that you have failed. And if you do achieve it, the success will be an anticlimax.

SETTING YOUR BUSINESS GOALS

Having a clear vision for your business, supported by a well-researched business plan, makes the difference between building a business and building a profitable business – provided the strategy is sound.

Setting clear business goals that you want to achieve within a defined period of time brings focus to the decisions you make every day. Having specific goals also enables you to monitor your achievements over a period of time so that you can measure the extent of your success.

Ask yourself quickly, on a scale of 1 to 10: '*Where am I in terms of knowing my short-, mid- and long-term goals?*'

- In three months
- In six months
- In one year
- In three years
- In 5 years and beyond

Many business owners do not give themselves time to focus fully on their mid- to long-term goals and will get stuck in a period of 'drift' that may slow growth and crush the sense of business vitality. Every project or business needs to maintain momentum. If you are unsure where you are headed, make time to 'Look Back From the Future' (see page 86).

Consider your future aims in terms of:

- Product or service range
- Source of supply
- Revenue
- Turnover
- Profitability
- Number of clients or customers
- Market level
- Your work hours
- Employees: whether full-time, part-time, outsourcing, associates etc

- Your location: whether in rented premises, home-based, serviced offices etc
- Your long-term goal for the business

On the basis of each of your replies, ask yourself:

'What is my immediate priority?

'What ACTION am I going to take today?'

On a scale of 1 to 10:

- How much closer to your goal will this action take you?
- How much further away will it take you?
- Should I Do it! or should I Ditch It?

Having a clear plan that is regularly revised and revisited will make day-to-day decision-making much easier.

- Action: if you feel too far out of your comfort zone and verging on the edge of panic, turn to page 22 and choose to enter your stretch zone.
- Action: DISCover other perspectives so that you feel fully prepared for the actions you are taking, using the DISC walk coming up on page 144.

PLANNING YOUR BUSINESS

Making clear decisions about your goals will help you to decide on the ideal business structure for your venture, at different stages of your business development. If you keep the future in mind as you focus on the present, you will be more likely to make decisions that lead you consistently in the right direction.

Typically, many business owners start out as sole traders,

and later on decide whether to become a limited company or a partnership. The size of the market and the number of people able to deliver the result will determine how big and how fast you can grow.

If you are already set up in business you may not need my insights into business structure at this point. If you are just starting out and want advice, the wisest place to begin is by talking to your bank manager. All of the high street banks provide some form of business start-up pack. A reputable accountancy firm will also be a valuable ally, and there are many government-supported resources available to offer advice on running, managing and financing business growth. (Further Resources offers a starting point for contact details).

 **DO IT!**

START-UP ESSENTIALS FOR SUCCESS IN BUSINESS

Whether you are a sole trader, a limited company or a partnership, there are certain business essentials to be stamped in your passport before you enter new territory.

1. **Never set up in business without first creating a business plan.** A business plan will keep you on track and keep you focused on your original start-up aims. The more time and consideration you give to creating a realistic and accurate plan of your business strategy, financial investment, cash flow, sales, marketing and supply chain, the more likelihood you have of long-term success. Thousands of businesses falter because people haven't paid enough attention to the planning stage.

2. **Always do your market research thoroughly.** Achieve this by gathering information on your competitors and asking potential customers what they want. No matter how well you think you

know what your customers *need*, the chances are you have more to learn about what they actually *want*.

3. **Get your pricing right.** Pay attention to your costings and make sure you account for overheads and your personal time when assessing your pricing strategy (see Step 5: HOW? for more about sales and marketing).

4. **Budget carefully.** Always keep a tight rein on the money and make sure you have enough financial contingency to see you through a slow patch. Under-capitalisation during the first year will claim many an unsuspecting business owner (see Step 6: HOW MUCH? for more about finance).

5. **Take advice from those in the know.** Experience counts for a lot. Always try to ask the advice of those who have got their ideas off the ground – or have helped others to make their business work. People who are successful usually know how to make sound business decisions, and they are often prepared to share their experience. Your bank manager and your accountant will also have a vested interest in helping you to succeed and will have a wealth of experience from working with other businesses.

6. **Invest in your personal development.** Find a business mentor who can help you avoid pitfalls and give you sound business advice. A good mentor is successful in business and emotionally objective, so he or she can help you to plan your way out of trouble before it hits or be ready to seize a new opportunity when it presents itself.

7. **Commit to following your business plan.** Once the plan is realistic in its aims, it will become your anchor, your benchmark for testing whether something is right or wrong for your business strategy. The plan is an active document that will keep you on track and prevent you from spending too much money upfront on non-essentials.

8. **Focus on your cash flow.** Cash is king in business. You need to manage your finances as is if your life depends upon it –

because it does. If you are unfamiliar with how a profit and loss sheet works, or you find yourself procrastinating rather than monitoring your cash flow on a regular basis, hire help now. Cash-flow problems are a serious threat to businesses of any size, especially during the start-up phase.

9. **Test the market.** Never make assumptions about your market, your competitors or pricing.

10. **Think 'sales' at all times.**

HOW TO GET OUT OF YOUR OWN WAY

There are two kinds of obstacles in business: the ones that we have no control over and the ones that we create ourselves. My philosophy is simple: there is no point in worrying about the things we have no control over. Instead, the way forward is to focus on what we can influence and, in so doing, get out of our own way.

Signs that you are in your own way include phrases such as:

- *'I would/should but ...'*
- *'I can't because ...'*
- *'I want to but ...'*
- *'Maybe next month/week/year'*
- *'I think I might ...'*

When we find ourselves putting things off, drifting rather than planning, heading back towards Brian Tracy's 'Someday Isle' (see page xxv), it is a clear sign that the thought of taking action is leaving you stranded in your panic zone (see page 22). You may feel you *need* to take that first step, but you don't yet *want* to. It's time to DISCover what is holding you back.

> **'You may feel you *need* to take that first step, but you don't yet *want* to.'**

DISCover NEW PERSPECTIVES

We all have strengths and weaknesses and a preferred pace of action, but we can also choose to adopt a different stance by stepping into other people's shoes and looking at a situation from a new perspective. Thinking things through in new and unfamiliar but productive ways can motivate us to take appropriate action to maintain momentum. The DISC approach is ideal for this.

The exercise below can be used in any decision-making situation. It raises self-awareness and involves consciously adopting the thinking of each of the DISC styles in turn (see Chapter 3 for a reminder of your own style). You can experience what it is like to respond to a situation as a 'High' D, I, S, or C style. With practice, this can become an invaluable tool as you can choose to 'raise' your awareness of each area.

For example, many leaders and sales people are High-D and High-I in approach, with a tendency to be fast-paced and verbal. They may get very enthusiastic about things and tend to say 'yes' first and worry about the detail later. I am one of them. The advantage of understanding DISC is that if I need to read through a contract or a written report I can tell myself to 'raise my C skills' in order to get into the right mindset for the task; or 'raise my S-style' if I need to listen to someone who is in distress.

I encourage my clients to get to know the DISC profiles of everyone they work with. Our own workspace is organised so that we sit in combinations that play to our strengths and increase productivity. For example, my finance controller, Syed Shoaib, has both C and S traits. He is excellent at what he does. He is also highly risk-averse and focused on the necessary detail of finance and business management. I deliberately sit

143

opposite him because he is my safeguard. His strengths allow me to play to mine – which limits the risk factor. I do nothing of any importance without running the figures past him first, and his knowledge enables me to make informed decisions. My D- and I-styles combined with his S- and C-styles provide both the accelerator and the brakes that balance the company. I can power forward with my foot on the accelerator confident that the brakes are in full working order and can be used to keep the business safe.

Likewise, I tend to keep the I-styles apart as they will distract each other with too much chat. An S-style can keep a C-style on track by asking them about delivery schedules. A D-style can help an S-style feel more comfortable with risk as he or she exposes them to a different way of thinking on a daily basis. It is a very dynamic and enriching way for a team to work together, which aids understanding and cuts down the tendency for people to criticise traits that are not a part of their own personality.

The DISC methodology is not a divination tool; it is a practical process that can reframe problem solving, communicating and making decisions. That is why I recommend a virtual DISCovery walk to help look at each important decision from every personal perspective.

If you are working in a team environment and have a good spread of DISC profiles among those you work with, simply ask each member of the team for their views from their own perspective. It is a very dynamic and equal form of team collaboration.

TAKE THE DISCovery WALK

This exercise is designed to help you see the world of business through the eyes of the other DISC styles. Taking the DISCovery walk will help you to look at your plan or your decision-making dilemma from each of the D, I, S, C perspectives. It gives you an objective overview and will offer new perspective on the kinds of thoughts and actions you need to take your plan forwards.

Walking your way through the four styles will give you a more balanced overview of your situation so that you are better placed to make a wise and effective decision.

- The D perspective will enable you to think big.
- The I perspective reminds you of who you know who can help to make things happen.
- The S perspective will keep things safe and prevent a high level of unnecessary risk.
- The C perspective keeps an eye on the detail and is a quality control.

D Think big	I Who do I know?
C Pay attention to the detail	S Make it safe

1. STEP INTO THE D-ZONE – WHERE EVERYTHING AND ANYTHING IS POSSIBLE

Stepping into the world of the D-style is your licence to think big. Whatever you are thinking now (if you are not a D), it means thinking even bigger than that. Ds are comfortable feeling uncomfortable. To the D-style, obstacles are a mere inconvenience and are a challenge to overcome.

D   Drive: *If you can dream it you can do it.*

Ask yourself the following questions in D-mode:
  'What would we do if we had no financial constraints?'
  'What would we do if we could not fail?'
  'If we were the BEST in the business what would our business look like?'
  *'If we were the BIGGEST in the business, what would our business
    look like?'*
  'What action will we need to take now?'

Now adopt the High-D approach to business planning:

Obstacles   Think of any challenges that may be ahead of you
         and in High-D mode; think of ways past, through
         or over or under them.

Conflict   Are there any conversations that you have been
         putting off? Think of yourself into High-D mode to
         decide what needs saying, to whom and when.

Tasks   Are there any actions that you have been putting
         off? Is there something standing in the way of you
         and success? Name it and *do it*, or delegate it, but
         get it behind you and do it now.

Decision-making style
Be focused, decisive and determined. There is no dwelling on past
mistakes.

2. WALK INTO THE I-ZONE – AND GET NETWORKING

I-styles are great communicators; they know lots of people and make friends easily. In this zone we are looking to join things up, in terms of finding people who can help you get where you want to go much faster. In this zone there is no room for shyness. I-styles have no problem asking a favour of a friend of a friend or approaching someone they don't even know.

> **I   Influence: *It's not* what *you know it's* who *you know.***

Ask yourself the following questions in I-mode:

'Who could we joint-venture with?' (those who share our client base but are not our competitors).

'Who do we know who could open doors for us?' (those who have effective contacts).

'Who do we know that we can call on to help us?'(those with the expertise you need).

'How will we tell people about our product/service?'(marketing).

'How can I use my influence now to increase our chances of success?'

Now adopt the High-I approach to business planning:

Networking   Make a list of who you know and how they might be able to help you, and think of ways that you may be able to help them. This is a two-way street.

Sales   I-styles often have many contacts in social media. How can you utilise social media to build connections and propel your business forward? Pick up the phone to make that call and start to connect the dots and get the picture.

Team building   Focus on those around you. Praise and encourage them so that they know how appreciated they are. Decide to arrange some social events to increase camaraderie.

> ### Decision-making style
> Be flexible in approach, enthusiastic about results and allow for variations in the final result.

3. TAKE THE PATH TO THE S-ZONE – AND CREATE HARMONY

S-styles are great team players. They like to work and live in a harmonious environment and will see tasks through to completion. They value security highly. Even if they are involved in a high-risk business they will find a way of minimising their personal risk; for example, they may have money saved as a contingency in case of emergency.

> ### S   Steadiness: *Look before you leap.*

Ask yourself the following questions in S-mode:
  'What might go wrong?'
  'If things don't work out what do we stand to lose?'
  'What is the back-up plan?'
  'How can we reduce the risks?'

'What support do we need?'
'What action can I take now to minimise the risk of something going wrong?'

How to adopt the High-S approach to business planning:

Simplification Is there a way of simplifying the way something is done in your business? Take a closer look at your processes.

Caring for others Is there anyone who might be affected by your decision in a negative way? Are you rocking the boat without considering others?

Risk assessment What is your back-up plan? How can you minimise the risk? Do you really need to sign personal financial guarantees, or are there other options? List your liabilities and build a lifeboat. Expect the best but plan for the worst.

Decision-making style

Be cautious in approach, look to the future and make sure you have eliminated all unnecessary risks. Put a process in place to support your decision and ensure delivery of the final result.

4. STEP CAUTIOUSLY INTO THE C-ZONE – AND GET THINGS RIGHT

On this part of the journey Mr Spock rules with 'Vulcan' logic. There is no room for emotion, just fact and figures.

C Compliance: *The devil is in the detail.*

Ask yourself the following questions in C-mode:
   'What information do we need to make sure we get things right?'
   'What is our contingency plan?'
   'What contracts or legalities need to be in place?'
   'What technology will we need?'
   'What additional research do we need to do?'
   'Do the figures stack up?'
   'What action do I need to take now to increase the accuracy of the outcome?'

Now adopt the High-C approach to business planning:

Planning Have you mapped out every step of setting up this business? Is there anything you might have overlooked?

The competition Have you completed an extensive competitor analysis? Have you looked at the marketplace to make sure your product or service is viable?

Forecasting Have you been over-optimistic with forecasts? Make sure the money is not going to run out faster than you anticipate, leaving you high and dry.

Decision-making style

Put on the High-C hat and take a fresh look at your business idea and then criticise it. This may sound negative, but in looking for flaws you will find something to be refined and improved that will ensure a quality result.

Working with people whose working styles differ from your own can be a mutual challenge. Being able to see things from another person's viewpoint is an essential leadership skill. Many entrepreneurs are very driven, fast-paced, determined and have a laser-sharp focus. Adopting others' perspectives can increase understanding and improve communication. It helps leaders to appreciate other people's points of view and to modify their approach accordingly. At times, when you feel under pressure because you are finding it hard to communicate with someone on your team, the DISCovery walk can be a powerful way to gain perspective.

DO IT! OR DITCH IT CHECKLIST

WHERE?

What is the plan?

When you think about launching your business idea, how confident do you feel that your plan will carry you through? Do you feel well prepared or does it feel like a high-risk venture? Your feelings signpost your true level of preparedness and help you to assess whether you are ready to commit to your business idea.

Try using the simple scale that follows to assess your current state of mind and to see if you are ready to get started. Consider each phrase below and rate by marking where on the line your state of mind lies. Do you feel closer to the right-hand column or the left-hand column?

This exercise does not evaluate the plan itself. There are no 'good feelings' or 'bad feelings' and no rights or wrongs. It is a way to evaluate your frame of mind.

On balance, are you in a 'Do It!' frame of mind? Or is that critical voice inside your head suggesting you should 'Ditch It' because your plan will not support the idea?

CHECK YOUR MINDSET

On a scale of 1 to 10, how close are you to your goal?

1 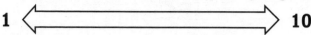 **10**

The 'Ditch It' Warning Signs	The 'Do It!' Mindset
There are gaps in our plan	We have covered all contingencies
Where are we headed?	We have a five-year plan
I don't trust my judgement	I trust our market research
The figures don't add up	Our accountant has checked the figures
The future is uncertain	We can adapt to market needs
Who will buy?	We already have some orders
How will we be found?	Our marketing strategy is working
I need to know more	We know enough to begin
I have serious doubts	I trust my judgement
What if we fail?	I can make this a success

WHAT ACTIONS WILL TAKE YOU ONE STEP CLOSER TO YOUR GOAL?

WRITE THEM HERE

STEP 4: WHO?

Who do you need to help you deliver?

PEROPLE POWER

'You can dream, create, design and build the most wonderful place in the world, but it requires people to make the dream a reality.'

Walt Disney

Step 4: WHO? considers the decisions we make that involve other people. Your business network ultimately determines your net worth.

Using DISC, you will find that people are different, but they are predictably different. Understanding how others tick, and helping them to work in roles that play to their strengths, will increase your chances of success because they will enjoy their work and be able to shine. Step 4 will help you to DISCover how to work better with other people, why conflict occurs, how to understand your customers and clients and how to hire your dream team to make your projects work. Your ability to adapt your management style to match the needs of the individual team members is your key to encouraging them to deliver their best results.

I have found that the positive business relationships I built in the early years have helped me to build my success as my businesses have grown. Many of my colleagues and associates are business friends as well as colleagues. I know I can count on them. Even when I have had to let people go I have tried to ensure that they know how much they were valued. Always show people respect in your business dealings.

Who can help you to turn your idea into action? How can you find people who are team players, who can act on their own initiative and who take pride in delivering quality work?

Building your dream team is like putting together your ideal partners for an adventurous expedition. Who do you *need* to take with you? Who do you *want* to be with you? Who may be awkward at times but a complete lifesaver when it matters? Climbing a mountain is only a good idea if you travel with people who know what to do, who remain unruffled under pressure or have climbed a few summits before. It becomes a very bad idea, liable to end in failure (or worse), if you attempt to climb solo, especially if you have no experience of the climatic conditions. Whether or not your business provides a specialist service, it makes sense to ensure you are supported by those who know what you are doing.

People are the front line of any business – and the most important asset, as the front line has a direct impact on the bottom line. Success is usually achieved more quickly and effectively in partnership with others, which is why the 'people' decisions that you make are so important. Not only do you need your team to have the appropriate professional skills, you will also want to ensure that you are building a team of people who will work effectively together and on whom you can rely, whether they are employed full time, under short-term contract or as a team of associates. Step 4 is therefore about WHO you need on your dream team and how to work with them.

> **'People are different – but they are predictably different.'**
>
> *Dr Sanford Kulkin*

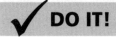 **DO IT!**

PENNY POWER KNOWS THE VALUE OF BUSINESS RELATIONSHIPS

Penny Power, founder and MD of Ecademy, has this to say about building business relationships:

> 'People who are being driven by fear, rush, and do not spend enough time building supportive relationships around them. They repel people with their desire to achieve a return on investment from every conversation. Your biggest asset will be the social capital you build around your business, on and offline. If you are known for the right reasons but not liked by enough people then you will achieve very little depth in your "following". This will damage your long-term success. Take time to love your business and what it does for others. Focusing on sales makes you a salesperson; focusing on building business relationships makes you a business owner.'

HOW TO CREATE YOUR DREAM TEAM

Creating a business that grows and expands to the point where you need to hire assistance is very exciting, but it can also be daunting. The thought of hiring and managing staff is enough to put some people off the idea of going into business in the first place. Every employer wants to 'hire right the first time' because it saves time, energy and resources. And it can be done – if you do it right and prepare in advance.

My own approach, especially when starting up something new, is to retain flexibility and to outsource as many tasks as possible until I am certain of the skills I need to help me deliver results.

It is easy to change suppliers if you need a different skill set. It is not so easy to make a change if you already have someone on the payroll.

The time to hire is when you have reached a point where someone could do the task you are doing – and possibly more cheaply – because you want to free up your time to do something that will generate more money for the business. For example, if you spend hours each week tallying your accounts when your time could be better spent generating revenue through selling or marketing, it is time to consider taking on a bookkeeper. This may be on a permanent or freelance basis.

A decision to employ someone permanently usually means finding someone with a different skill set to your own. This is an important point, because they may have a different working style from yours as well. Most of us prefer to be surrounded by like-minded people, but it pays to be task-led first and people-orientated second when it comes to deciding what is best for your business.

The DISC model (see Chapter 3 for a reminder) comes into its own here. At its core is an appreciation of the differences between us and how acceptance of and respect for those differences can enable people to work together and improve decision-making. A healthy business needs people with the skills to deliver effectively across all key areas, from sales to finance, from planning to purchasing and project management and so on. It also needs people who are working in roles that they enjoy, because that will help to ensure they deliver their best work. Even a skilled all-rounder will enjoy doing some tasks more than others. The DISC model helps to clarify the character traits you ideally need within your company to balance those you already have.

Now would be a good time to go through the DISC questionnaire (see page 56) to find out your own dominant traits, if you have not already done so. As a reminder: D-style and C-style people are task-orientated, whereas High I-style and S-style people are more people-orientated. If your profile shows you to be I- or S-style, you may want to consider asking someone with more D and C traits to join you at interview to help gain a balanced view.

HOW TO DECIDE WHO TO HIRE

I want to share some simple strategies for successful people-preneurship that we all know in theory but that we may forget to apply in practice. To identify the skills you need within your business, begin by asking yourself some core questions:

'What does the business do well?'

'What could it be better at?'

'Where is it losing out to competitors?'

'Where do I need some help to deliver our product or service more effectively?'

'Who has those skills?'

'How can I make sure I can attract the best person for the job?'

Hiring may mean taking someone on, on a freelance, temporary or permanent basis, but whatever the arrangement, I always use DISC personality profiling before I make a hiring decision so that I can be sure I am matching their personality to the needs of the business. The reality is that no one will change their personality to suit the job; they will try to change the job to suit their personality. For example, if a job requires somebody to focus on research and detail, but they are more people- than task-orientated, then they will look for opportunities to wander about: making cups of coffee, photocopying, attending meetings; doing anything that offers social interaction and allows them to talk.

> **'The reality is that no one will change their personality to suit the job; they will try to change the job to suit their personality.'**

The following summary is a reminder of the core positive traits of each of the DISC styles and the pressure points that may cause friction when teams are working under pressure.

D

High D-styles have the gift of confident decision-making.

Decide with confidence:

- Focus on tasks.
- Will take calculated risks.
- Will go it alone if necessary.
- Will go against the pack.
- Want instant results.
- Action-orientated.
- Will take action if they know *why*; they will work out the *how* later.
- Have self-belief.
- Like change.
- The bigger the challenge the greater the motivation.

CLICK OR CLASH?

Watch out for: arrogant or overbearing attitude; an inability to listen.

I

High I-styles have the gift of communication.

Network naturally:

- Who can I ask for advice?
- What networking groups would be useful?
- Who can I partner with?
- Who can help promote my business?
- Who can I connect with to keep me on track?
- Who has done this before and what can I learn from them?
- How can we make it fun?
- How will we celebrate our success?

CLICK OR CLASH?

Watch out for: exaggerated claims or evasive answers.

C

C-styles have the gift of analytical thinking.

Logic rules:

- Do the numbers add up?
- Has enough research been done on the market size?
- Has a full competitor analysis been completed?
- What is a realistic time frame for launching the business?
- Can technology be used to support the business and minimise costs?
- What are the legal requirements?

CLICK OR CLASH?

Watch out for: pedantic approach; aloofness; critical; rigidity in approach.

S

S-styles have the gift of keeping things safe and secure.

Keep it safe:

- What is my back-up plan?
- How can I do this and not risk my security?
- Who could be affected if things go wrong?
- Who can I turn to for support and guidance?
- What organisations will be able to help?
- Resist change.

CLICK OR CLASH?

Watch out for: stubborn, passive/aggressive posture.

An interview or selection process takes place over a number of stages, but there is rarely any obligation to go through all stages with inappropriate candidates if you have short-listed effectively in the early stages.

Job interview

1. CV/résumé submitted.
2. Telephone interview.
3. First interview.
4. Second interview.
5. Job offer.
6. Induction.

If you and your team have prepared in advance, it should be possible to see clearly who are the most appropriate candidates and which applications can be 'ditched' at an early stage.

HOW TO PREPARE TO HIRE

Preparation is everything, in hiring as in every other aspect of running a business. Before you take anybody new on board for your business, whether permanently or as a business associate, it is wise to have properly considered:

- What skills and traits you have in your business – and what you now need.
- Key interview questions that will get to the heart of candidates' motivation.

The following Person Specification Sheet is typical of the kind that human resources departments everywhere will use. No matter how resistant you are to form - filling, it is extremely useful to complete something like this before you write one word of an advert for the job, and before you begin the interview process. It will help you to clarify not only what you need but also what you don't need from your candidates.

Person Specification Sheet

Criteria	Essential	Desirable
Qualifications		
Experience		
Skills required		
Personal characteristics		
Behaviours		

Job specification

It is vital to list the following in order to match the job task to the individual – as we have already discussed, people don't change their personality to suit the job, they attempt to change the job to suit their personality. Producing a 'match list' will be an invaluable guide for you.

Overall purpose of the job:

Key Tasks:

1.

2.

3.

4.

5.

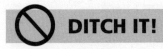 **DITCH IT!**

THE COMMON MISTAKES THAT PEOPLE MAKE WHEN HIRING

1. **Lack of advance preparation.** It is important to prepare a job description for the role, and to know the skills you will require, before you place the advert or start to interview. The recruitment process is time-consuming and all too often staff or help are hired simply because someone is 'there', rather than because they are the best person for the job. A job description will help you to decide who to employ. Sticking to a list of interview questions prepared in advance will help you to consider and compare everyone on an equal footing.

2. **CV fatigue.** Some job adverts will generate hundreds of replies, and sorting through the applications can become overwhelming. It is helpful to have a checklist of the skills that are required, but trust your instincts, too. If necessary, make use of a recruitment consultancy to take the strain and help with selection and interviewing.

3. **Making do.** Warning: if you find yourself trying to talk yourself into hiring someone, STOP. Even if you need someone to start working for you straight away, resist the temptation to hire interviewees simply because they turned up on the day. It is better to keep recruiting until you find the right person. Remember, too, to check all references.

4. **Repeating past mistakes.** If you have hired people previously and you are suffering from high turnover of staff, it is important to find out why they are deciding to leave. It doesn't matter whether you have one or 101 employees: you need your staff to be onside and happy. An 'exit interview' or questionnaire can be very revealing and helpful to the future of your company. You may need to reassure your employee that their comments will not jeopardise their chance of a future reference, though.

5. **Selecting solely on personality.** Having a working rapport is important, but no matter how well you get on with someone you need also to make sure they are going to have the right skill set for the job.

6. **Recruiting in your own image.** *'I don't know what it is, but there is something about this person that I really like!'* Time and time again I find business owners who have recruited people just like them. It's OK if that's what you really need, but quite often you require someone a bit different to add to your dream team.

'Do or Ditch, but don't make do.'

BUILDING A TEAM

Team training and regular meetings create enthusiasm and, if run well, can ensure everyone is pulling in the same direction towards the goal of the company. Take the decision early on to consciously communicate with your team and to get to know them and trust them to do a good job.

Ask members of your team, 'What parts of your job do you really love? If there was something else to take on – what would it be?' Involve them in assessing the requirements of the department when appropriate to do so and bear in mind the needs of the future. When you give the power back to those who are doing the work, they are less likely to resist doing new tasks and more likely to tune in to the commercial concerns of the business; but beware – sometimes ten people can have ten different opinions and stalemate or frustration results.

The slippery slope to low morale is a very fast one in comparison to the time it takes to build the team back up again; therefore, it is worth planning ahead to safeguard the wellbeing of the team as much as possible. This goes beyond the processes and procedures that the company will have in place to ensure that the recommended processes and legalities are followed.

In a *work* environment:

A **D-style** (Dominant) person is motivated by results and has a fear of failure, so give them challenging but achievable targets. They often like to be judged by results rather than methods, and resist being micro-managed. *Is this you?*

An **I-style** (Influential) person will thrive on public praise and recognition. The challenge can be keeping to deadlines as they can easily get distracted or can see many different ways to deliver the end result, and may continually change their mind after making a decision. Make sure there is follow-up and a completion date. *Is this you?*

An **S-style** (Steady) person needs time to adapt to change, and wants to make sense of the process, so take the time to explain why any change is necessary. Ask them for their thoughts and acknowledge how they may be feeling. Their decisions may be based on the needs of others. *Is this you?*

A **C-style** (Compliant) person will be concerned about what may have been overlooked, so invite them to look into the detail. They may be slower to make decisions because they will want to ensure that everything has been considered and all is correct before committing to an outcome. *Is this you?*

DISCover WHAT MAKES YOUR TEAM TICK

D TASK-DRIVEN/Outgoing	**I PEOPLE-DRIVEN**/Outgoing
DRIVING PASSION: WINNING	DRIVING PASSION: RECOGNITION
GREATEST FEAR: BEING TAKEN ADVANTAGE OF	**GREATEST FEAR: LOSS OF POPULARITY**
COMFORT ZONE: Prefers – Directing others Fast decisions Looking at the big picture	**COMFORT ZONE:** Prefers – Collaborating with others Win-win decisions There are always other options
DECISION-MAKING TRAITS: Proactive Clear-thinking Strategic	**DECISION-MAKING TRAITS:** Proactive Changes their mind Creative
KEY QUESTION: Will this help me to hit my target?	**KEY QUESTION:** How will it help the business to stand out?
UNDER PRESSURE: Finds comfort in taking action Puts self and others under pressure Becomes even more directive May act before thinking	**UNDER PRESSURE:** Finds comfort in talking Could talk rather than take action Looks for other options Gets distracted
CLICK OR CLASH? Will click with all styles if everything is on target Will clash: With other D-styles unless there is mutual respect With I-styles if there is too much talk and not enough action With S-styles if there is resistance to change With C-styles if the need for detail holds things up	**CLICK OR CLASH?** Will click with all styles if they are liked by them Will clash: With D-styles if they show public hostility towards them or stop the 'fun approach' With other I-styles if they compete for centre stage With S-styles if they can't be persuaded With C-styles if they always stick rigidly to the rules

C TASK-DRIVEN/ Reserved

DRIVING PASSION: PERFECTION

GREATEST FEAR: GETTING IT WRONG

COMFORT ZONE:
Prefers –
Working alone
Logical decisions
Checking the detail
Gathering information

DECISION-MAKING TRAITS:
Plans ahead to avoid problems
Perfectionist
Decides via a process of elimination

KEY QUESTION:
How will this ensure efficiency?

UNDER PRESSURE:
Finds comfort in the detail
Can suffer from paralysis of analysis

CLICK OR CLASH?
Will click with all styles if their views are listened to
Will clash:
With D-styles if they disregard concerns
With I-styles if they ignore the need for detail
With S-styles if they won't see the need for change
With other C-styles if they clash on the interpretation of the detail

S PEOPLE-DRIVEN/ Reserved

DRIVING PASSION: HARMONY

GREATEST FEAR: CHANGE/LOSS OF SECURITY

COMFORT ZONE:
Prefers –
Working in harmony
Planned safety-focused decisions
Familiarity, with no surprises
Tried and tested methods

DECISION-MAKING TRAITS:
Safety and security
Likes clarity of purpose
Will ask and involve others

KEY QUESTION:
How will it help the business to run smoothly and safely?

UNDER PRESSURE:
Finds comfort in working with a team
May withdraw to avoid conflict

CLICK OR CLASH?
Will click with all styles if everything is stable and harmonious
Will clash:
With D-styles if change happens too quickly
With I-styles if they are over-optimistic
With other S-styles – they are less likely to clash openly
With C-styles if procrastination affects security

DISCover HOW YOU COMMUNICATE

The reasons why we 'click or clash' in our personal or business life are often to do with our style of communication. Do you recognise the DISC styles among those you know? The pressure points tend to occur when we try to communicate in a style that the other person finds hard to understand. For example, if a D-style person makes pronouncements without listening to others' feedback; if an I-style person talks about themselves too much; if an S-style becomes resistant to change; if a C-style presents information using excessive detail. If you understand where the potential tension points are, you can begin to manage situations more effectively in the workplace.

D	I
High D-styles are very direct communicators. They 'tell it how it is' and do not always take account of others' feelings	High I-styles love to talk They will enthuse, chat, banter, and love talking about themselves, tell stories
Style of speech: Direct, to the point, tells	**Style of speech:** Friendly, flamboyant, sells
Phrases often used: I can, You can, Why not? When? Why don't you? What is the main issue? The point is, Trust me	**Phrases often used:** We can, I did, You can, Me too, It'll be OK, No problem
C	**S**
C-styles encourage in-depth analysis They want to understand why something is as it is	S-styles seek reassurance. They use the language of routine and security
Style of speech: Detailed, factual, logical	**Style of speech:** Reassuring, calm, considered
Phrases often used: Why? What if? The options are, I will look into it, I have written it down, The facts are, Research states that …	**Phrases often used:** How? How are you? We usually, We always, Talk to me, I am listening, In the past we used to

Adapt your style

Focus on communicating with your team members in a way that reflects their personal style. Are they detail-orientated? Give them facts and figures to help them plan and complete their task. Are they results-orientated? Give them a target and reward them with status. Are they warm and outgoing? They will be motivated by praise and appreciation. Are they methodical? Make sure there is a clear process in place for them to follow.

Encourage feedback

Encourage your people to communicate with you as part of their development: 'Tell me what you need', 'Tell me your ideal solution', 'If this was your business, what would you do?' Suggest they ask each other for feedback: 'What do you think?', 'What do you suggest?' Asking for their views can make people feel more valued and can help you with your own decisions.

- Encourage mutual respect.
- Help individuals to appreciate each other's differences and you will build a team that delivers results. Those who work together effectively will also come up with the most efficient solutions.

Meet each team member on a one-to-one basis

Though you lead a team, you manage individuals. An effective manager will have the ability to make each member of staff feel as if they are uniquely appreciated. It is useful to set aside time to speak to team members on a one-to-one basis. This is especially important if you are planning to make an announcement. It is a high-risk strategy to announce major news to a group without having briefed them as individuals in advance.

D-styles tend to be more vocal than others: you will always know what they think – they will tell you. C-styles, who are less extrovert, may feel it is inappropriate to speak up, or may dislike voicing their opinions in front of a group. Often they will prefer to email or voice concerns in private. A one-to-one session with each member of the team will make them feel valued and allow them to raise concerns in confidence.

EFFECTIVE WAYS TO MANAGE YOUR TEAM

The best way to build your team and to get people to focus on the future is to let them talk, let them know you are listening and share your plans for the future.

Keep everyone on track

One of the habits I have found most effective is to email a 'Monday message' to all staff each week, to frame the week ahead positively. It is a simple template that takes very little time to complete, but it tells people: this is what we achieved last week; these are the highlights; this week we're aiming for Y and we are focusing on X. I try to keep it light and often add an inspiring quote or an uplifting piece of news. It helps people to focus on their immediate priorities, reflect on achievements and feel appreciated.

Nip gossip in the bud

Rumour and idle gossip can derail, disrupt and undermine a business. The best way to make sure that it is nipped in the bud – or, better still, doesn't start in the first place – is to encourage a culture of fairness and openness and to make sure that you keep communicating with your team.

Add a social element

Few people work solely for money. Most people enjoy their work because they enjoy their work environment and the company of colleagues. Setting up a social occasion now and then will help your team to feel appreciated and will encourage people to bond. It allows business owners and managers to get to know their staff on a more informal basis, too. Of course, be sensitive to the age range of your team, or cultural and social differences. Ask people for suggestions; but your choices need to match the character of your staff and also to meet the needs of your budget.

Encourage people to take responsibility
Ask people for their recommendations and support them in their wish to do things their way – but with guidance. Introduce the Do It! or Ditch It decision-making tools as a part of everyday strategy so that there is a structured approach to taking action and monitoring progress.

Examine under-performance
Look for the reasons behind poor performance and use the three 'R's: Remotivate, Retrain or Replace.

Tolerate mistakes
Mistakes are an important part of the learning process – at every level. Few entrepreneurs make a success of their business without making some errors along the way. If something goes wrong it is important first to ask 'Why?' Could procedures be improved? Is someone overloaded? Why did the mistake happen? What mechanisms and safeguards need to be put into place to prevent it happening again? If you ask the person who made the mistake for a solution, they will probably know exactly what is needed, and take greater ownership of the task in future.

Avoid a 'blame' culture
There is a management truism that states: 'Every time you point your finger at someone, there are probably three fingers pointing back at you.' The first thing I always do when something

goes wrong is to consider, 'How did I contribute to that?' 'Did I communicate as effectively as I could have?' There is another saying that I have found to be true: 'The effectiveness of your communication is the response you get.'

Generally, I have found that people who make mistakes, and who care that they have made a mistake, will rarely make the same mistake again. The trick is to work together to *make sure* it never happens again. As Thomas J. Watson, the founder of IBM, is credited as saying after an employee had made an expensive mistake:

'I was asked if I was going to fire an employee who made a mistake that cost the company $600,000. No, I replied, I just spent $600,000 training him. Why would I want somebody to hire his experience?'

If mistakes are made consistently, then a decision to let someone go may have to be made, but in the big scheme of things if you are generally happy with your employee or freelance the cost of retraining someone new may outweigh the cost of the short-term error.

MAKING PEOPLE FEEL VALUED

A common mistake when creating a new business venture is to put all the emphasis on boosting sales and not enough time on building morale. Be warned: a team begins the day you hire someone. Making people feel valued, secure, liked, giving them clear objectives and explaining where they fit into your priorities will put you on track for the future.

If you anticipate people's fears and anxieties, and make sure they have the skills and support to do their job well, as well as making clear what the company's future needs and priorities are likely to be, they will want to do the best they can.

Building a working team that you can rely upon to get the job done and also enjoy working with is the aim of every business owner. A good team is stronger than any individual and can make things happen in new and creative ways; so, if a key team member leaves, it can be highly disruptive to everyone else as well. Many businesses will trace the loss of several key members of staff to the departure of one key player. This is true of those within your freelance teams as well.

People are loyal to people, not to businesses. I often say to businesses that have a high turnover of staff, 'How can you expect your customers to remain loyal to you, if your staff aren't?' If you have regular clients but every time they contact your company there's somebody new on the telephone, it doesn't reflect well on you or your business.

Don't wait to let things get to the stage where someone wants to resign before you decide to do something about it. By that stage, even if you succeed in getting them to change their mind, it will never be quite the same. Rather like ending a relationship or selling your house, once someone has decided to let go, the chances are that they will no longer feel the same level of attachment to your business, and you may no longer feel the same degree of trust or commitment.

A new recruit may work at only 50 per cent capacity for the first three to six months. A demotivated employee may function at 50 per cent or less for six months or more before they finally resign. That represents twelve months of lost work and lost revenue. Guard against this by maintaining the motivation of your team and keeping them involved in the goals of the business.

DO IT!

TOP TIPS FOR RETAINING YOUR KEY PLAYERS

Give thanks where it is due

When was the last time you told those you work with how valuable they are? Do you make a habit of making them feel appreciated and saying: 'Thank you, well done'?

D-style business owners are often reluctant to praise people because they expect them to start asking for more money. The reality is that most people appreciate being appreciated and recognised for the work they do. Tell a High I-style they have done well and they will walk through fire for you. They thrive on praise and wilt with criticism. The more public the praise the better they will like it. S-styles will feel good if *you* are feeling good and if they have helped something happen to the mutual benefit of all. C-styles, on the other hand, will prefer to be praised in private for a job well done. They will want to know what specifically they did right, so that they can repeat it.

Reward appropriately

Everyone on your team will probably be motivated by something different. If you run a small team, it can be invaluable to take time to find the right reward for the right person.

Distance working

If your team is off-site or self-employed, you can still show your appreciation. Someone may have gone the extra mile to help you to deliver on a project; they may have deferred their fee because they know you are waiting for payment from a client; perhaps they have introduced you to some valuable contacts; or simply been there throughout the growth of your business. Whatever it is –

make sure they know that you recognise the part they have played and that they know you will reciprocate. If you don't want to lose your best people to your competitors, be aware of how valuable they are to you, and make sure they know that you know it, too.

Make sure people enjoy their work

A football manager's place is on the touchline. He's not running onto the pitch and scoring goals. If you put people in the right positions you should be able to stay off the pitch and let them do their job. Monitor and measure performance – but allow people to do their jobs.

HOW TO MANAGE STRESS AT WORK

It's frustrating to hear managers express sentiments such as 'You just can't get the people these days', 'It would be better for everyone if he/she left', 'People just don't care'. It's nonsense, of course; people do care – but they need to know that the management cares about them, too – and that means protecting and looking out for your team when they are under pressure.

Read the pressure gauge

Workplace stress and burnout are major costs to businesses and individuals, but they are avoidable. I talk to my team daily to stay tuned into their stress levels. I use the scale of 1 to 10 with them (see page 41) as a quick working tool to monitor current needs. Level 1 means 'I am not under pressure', level 10 means 'I am feeling totally overwhelmed'. I value this approach because it is fast and enables people to ask for help without them realising it.

Many employees find it very hard to say, 'I have got too much to do.' Fast-paced leaders may unwittingly create an environment that is perpetually at other people's levels 9 or 10. This can be a challenge for both managers and staff.

Most people can work at levels 8 or 9 for short periods. They are being stretched, but verging on overload. I always adjust the pressure at levels 8 and 9 because level 10 is a tipping point: the damage has already been done and your employee is potentially on the road to burnout. Take the pressure off by outsourcing the task or involving other employees to help with the workflow. Consider investing in a long-term hire if the workload is increasing permanently beyond the capacity of the role. Working at levels 9 and 10 is fine for short periods, but it depends on the number of hours worked and length of time the situation is likely to continue.

Decide to stretch your team's capabilities

The 1 to 10 scale is a useful immediate tool, but in the long term you want to be able to encourage people to grow, to take risks and to stretch their capabilities. Introducing the stretch zone model can be a very useful tool for helping people to understand that short periods of 'discomfort' are a positive not a negative experience.

Don't dump, delegate

When you become overstretched, don't dump, delegate. It is unwise to give detailed work to a big-picture person, or strategic tasks to someone who will get stuck in the detail. If there is any question of your existing staff dropping the ball or making mistakes, consider outsourcing the role for a period of time.

Consider outsourcing

Outsourcing key tasks has several benefits. A new team member can lift morale and bring new energy to the workplace; outsourcing is a way of testing someone out before you take them on board; it is an effective use of resources, as an outsourced worker will not cost you the same in terms of overheads; it is easy to cancel the arrangement if their approach to the job is not a good 'fit'; it can allow other members of the team to adjust more comfortably to their new roles and responsibilities. Building a network of external resources allows a flexible and creative approach to delivering the outcome you need, especially when your team is overloaded.

INVEST IN YOUR OWN DEVELOPMENT

People think nothing of investing in new technology or training new staff – but they rarely acknowledge that they have a skill gap themselves. When I ask business owners about the amount invested in their business in the last twelve months, I am told about computer systems, software upgrades, photocopiers, staff training and so on. *What is missing is their investment in themselves.* The reasons given are rarely to do with money – or even time. They simply have not thought about it or don't really see the value in it. But personal development for you as a business *owner* is a must as part of your annual budget.

Self-development because is a fundamental principle that I absolutely believe in and I would strongly urge everyone in business to follow suit. It doesn't have to cost a fortune. There are any number of styles and types of resource available:

- Listen to audio CDs in the car.
- Read autobiographies by those who have 'made it'.
- Read business books and magazines.
- Network and attend business seminars.
- Watch online training videos and talks.
- Find a business coach or mentor.

When you are looking at your skill set, do you need to develop your financial awareness in business? Do you need to be more aware of social media? Do you need to be more aware of how the web can work for you? If you look at your personal characteristics, do you need to develop more drive, more positivity? Do you need to develop your communication skills, your people skills, your management skills?

Investing in your own development creates value for the long term. You will remain your greatest asset.

> *'If you're ripe you rot and if you are green you grow.'*

DO IT! OR DITCH IT CHECKLIST

WHO?

People power

Who have you got on board to help you to make your business run smoothly? Are you trying to do everything yourself or do you feel well supported by others who have a range of valuable expertise? Knowing that you are not 'going it alone' will help you to assess whether you are ready to turn your idea into action.

Using the simple scale that follows, you can assess your current state of mind to see whether you are ready to hire others. Consider each characteristic and rate by marking where on the line your state of mind lies. Do you feel closer to the right-hand column or the left-hand column?

This exercise does not evaluate your idea itself. There are no 'good feelings' or 'bad feelings' and no rights or wrongs. It is a way to evaluate your frame of mind.

On balance, are you in a 'Do It' frame of mind? Or is that critical voice inside your head suggesting you should 'Ditch It' because your support network is not strong enough?

CHECK YOUR MINDSET

On a scale of 1 to 10, how close are you to your goal?

1 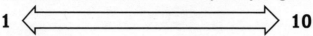 **10**

The 'Ditch It' Warning Signs	The 'Do It!' Mindset
I am going it alone	I have a strong support network
You can't get good staff	I can train people up
It's quicker to do it myself	I need people with complementary skills
I don't trust my people skills	I will get some help with interviewing
Recruitment costs money	Outsourcing is cost-effective
What if someone leaves?	Incentives will encourage staff to stay
I need to feel in control	Delegation is a strong point
Joint ventures are time-consuming	I will joint-venture with others to increase profile
What if we fail?	We plan to succeed
I dread being a manager	I will invest in my own development too

WHAT ACTIONS WILL TAKE YOU ONE STEP CLOSER TO YOUR GOAL?

WRITE THEM HERE

STEP 5: HOW?

How will you achieve your goal?

SALES AND MARKETING

*'"Well done is better than well said": what action
do you need to take today?'*

Benjamin Franklin

Step 5: HOW? uses the Do It! or Ditch It techniques to improve sales and marketing, helping you to turn your customers' needs into those all-important wants. Sales and marketing are the HOW of business decision-making. They are the route to your customers, who determine the profitability of your business.

Beware the danger zone: a lot of resources can be wasted on marketing if the initial goal is not clear enough. Even more can be wasted if you have invested too much time in developing the perfect product, but have no one to sell it to, and no distribution in place. The cliché is true. Time is money in business. Deciding on a marketing plan and spending time and effort into putting your strategy into practice is all-important. *Do* do your market research properly at the outset – and do make sure you have a route to market. *Ditch* the idea of waiting until something is perfect before you start selling. Feedback from the marketplace at an early stage is crucial to your success.

The good thing about running a small business is the level of flexibility that you have and the speed with which you can make decisions. The fewer people involved in making any kind of decision, the more quickly and easily things can be turned around. Big corporations are like large tankers – it takes a long time to turn them around. A small business is like a motorboat: pacy and easy to manoeuvre.

As you stand at the helm of your business, your marketing strategy turns the wheel that will steer you in the direction of your business plan. An effective marketing campaign has immense power. It has the capacity to turn moderately successful turnover into handsome profit; it can turn an invisible brand into a household name. The UK Chartered Institute of Marketing (CIM) sums up the purpose of marketing into a succinct phrase:

> ### *'Marketing is the management process that identifies, anticipates and satisfies customer requirements profitably.'*

Those three words 'identifies', 'anticipates' and 'satisfies' need to be at the heart of every decision that makes up the marketing strategy for your business. Marketing makes your product or service visible; it may make it appear more desirable; and it always needs to deliver a profitable return on investment.

The Do It! or Ditch It approach to decision-making in marketing is all about understanding your customer profile and ensuring that every decision you make is building your customer base and delivering a profitable result. Everything you do in sales and marketing should show a return on investment, whether you are giving your time or allocating spend. Focusing on *how* you will achieve your goal will help you to focus your time wisely and to ditch methods that are no longer working. *Testing and measuring* the results will ensure that you keep monitoring the return on investment and modify your approach as and when necessary.

Your marketing plan focuses on the bigger picture, so that when you are engrossed in the nitty-gritty of the day-to-day, you never forget what your priorities are. Sales and marketing delivers day-to-day turnover – and also contributes enormously to building your brand profile and achieving your long-term objectives.

In my experience most start-ups spend the majority of their time perfecting a product and don't spend enough time on thinking about how they market the product. A product without distribution is a disaster and will lead to broken dreams.

> **'A product without distribution is a disaster and will lead to broken dreams.'**

SELL, SELL, SELL

The number one skill needed by any successful entrepreneur is the ability to sell. To be a success you need to become a sales *master*. Many of the people who go on BBC's *Dragons' Den* are inventors. They give away equity in their business in return for expertise in business distribution. In most cases they also need help getting the product to market.

Today's business people need to teach tomorrow's generation three things if they are to succeed in business: to respect themselves; to respect others; and the skill of knowing how to sell.

Today's business people also need to help their own sales teams to do the best possible job, by sharing information.

> **'Remember: you can't hit a goal you can't see'**

Some companies will share information and others won't. But the reality is that sales teams need to know whether they have hit their monthly targets; they need to be free to discuss what has sold, what hasn't, and why. If you want to keep everyone in the company on board there needs to be transparency. Your team can't hit a goal that they can't see. My recommendation is always to encourage a culture of openness and transparency. Everyone should know: 'This is where we're going; this is what we're aiming for', so that everyone feels that they are in it together.

MARK RHODES' NUMBER ONE SALES TIP

Mark Rhodes built an Internet software company that provided for clients such as Body Shop, Virgin Cosmetics and Dorling Kindersley Publishers before selling it to a company in Silicon Valley in 2001. He is now a business mentor and speaker, specialising in helping businesses to optimise their results.

'They say the biggest problem in sales is that people don't ask for the sale, but the second-biggest problem is that people ask for the sale too soon. They ask before they know for certain that they have fully matched the benefits of their products or services to the potential client's needs. They also ask for the sale before they have built up credibility with the potential client.

If you have built the right level of credibility, demonstrated the added value and matched that to the goals of the potential client, then the deal should close naturally with little prompting. A soft approach that asks, "What would need to happen for us to work together on this?" can allow you to get additional information which will help you to move forward.'

Five tips for optimum pricing

- Don't underprice your product or service. Price is only *one* deciding factor for a customer.
- A price objection can obscure the real reasons your prospect is hesitating. They want to be sure they have the best deal.

- Every price is too high until your customer identifies why they want or need the goods.
- When your price is higher, you must provide extra value.
- People prefer to buy from people they like.

ONE: THE MOST DANGEROUS NUMBER IN BUSINESS

There is a number in business that is more dangerous than any other: the number one. When you have only one of something in business you become vulnerable. Whether it is one customer, one supplier, or one marketing method, one spells danger. For example, if you have only one client, you leave yourself wide open to problems if your contact leaves the company (and the Inland Revenue may view it as employed work, which could cause you problems); if you have only one supplier you have no flexibility concerning delivery, or room for negotiation on price; if you have only one source of administrative backup, you will be stymied if someone is ill. If you rely totally on your own knowledge and decisions there will be no room for flexibility in your approach and you will limit your potential for growth. Contingency and agility are important in business. Nothing is forever.

It is particularly dangerous to rely upon only one method of marketing, especially a new method of e-marketing. If you rely totally on the Internet for generating leads, what happens if the Internet goes down? If you put all your eggs in one basket, you will be in danger of forgetting the value of other methods of reaching your customers – and may miss a tranche of business completely.

BALANCING THE WHEELS OF MARKETING

If a vehicle is to stay on track, the wheels need to be balanced and in alignment. This is as important when directing your marketing strategy as it is when driving a car. Marketing is the vehicle you are using to deliver your product to market.

There is an activity that I often use to encourage business owners to consciously develop eight to ten different marketing methods, and to know what return these methods give to their business.

1. Take a moment to draw a circle and divide it into seven or more segments, like the spokes on a wheel.

2. Mark the centre of the circle, where the spokes cross, with a 0.

3. Mark the outer sections, where the spokes meet the perimeter of the circle, with 10.

4. In each of those slices write a different marketing method that you use for your business.

5. For example, Pay per Click, joint-venturing with another business, social media, client referral, telemarketing, email marketing, networking, PR, direct mail. Whatever it may be, write it down.

6. Next, score each spoke on a scale of 1 to 10, according to how well each method of marketing is working for you. Are you getting an appropriate return for your level of investment? In other words, is it delivering the results you expect? Are the results worth the amount you are spending? Is the quality of the result in line with your expectations?

If you are using the method and can assess it, mark it on a scale of 1 to 10.

If you're not using it at all then it is currently a zero.

If you have no idea whether the technique is working, then you can't score it at all. You need to do some investigation.

7. Once again, test and measure – especially if you are thinking of trying something new.

The scale of 1 to 10 will show your level of activity in each area and will give you a chance to decide whether you need to increase a level of activity in an area or change your marketing tactic.

In particular, be savvy about using digital marketing methods where results can be improved by changing key words and so on. Investing in getting expert advice in this area can keep you one step ahead of the market.

THE WHEELS OF MARKETING IN ACTION

John runs a national mail order company providing specialist plumbing supplies. He created a marketing wheel and marked it up as follows:

Segment 1: Pay per Click
I might mark this as a 7. We had 20,000 hits last month and I am satisfied with the level of results I am getting – but I would rather be paying less for the service.

Segment 2: Telemarketing
I might mark this as a 1. I used to use this technique a great deal – but not any more. Marking it as a 1 has prompted me to consider whether we could be doing more in this area.

Segment 3: Client referral
I have marked this as a 3. It is an area we could be doing a lot more with. We have a lot of regular customers, but we don't put much effort into asking them to refer us to other people.

We will start adding a note to our email sign-off to say, 'If you are satisfied with our service please tell other businesses. All successful referrals will be rewarded with a discount via our loyalty scheme.'

Segment 4: Advertising
This is a 0. We used to advertise in the trade press, but it was a high investment for very little return. These days it is easy to gain profile via other means, so I cut the budget completely. I am still happy with that decision.

Segment 5: PR

This is a 5. We have a very low level of activity in this area, but I contribute occasional articles to a trade journal. It is time-consuming, which is a disadvantage, but has proved valuable for profile, which has brought in new customers.

Segment 6: Joint-venturing

This is an 8. This style of marketing is effective for us. We have very effective working relationships with a reputable building supplier. However, we could do more and on a larger scale.

Segment 7: Social media

This is a 1 because we don't really know if we should or how we could make use of social media. More research and education is needed.

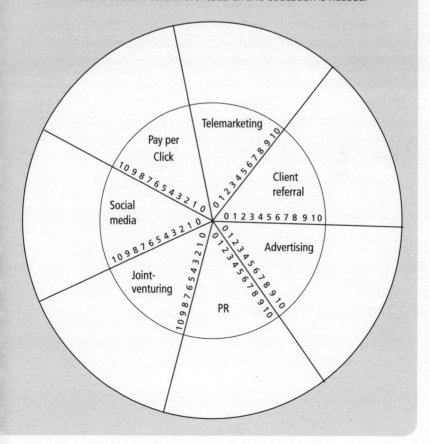

THE TIMES THEY ARE e-CHANGING

If your business has been established for a few years it is likely that the marketing methods you are using now are very different from when you first started. Sometimes it's good to think back to how you got your first customers. What marketing method did you use? Is it worth trying it again? Ten years ago a large proportion of your mailings would have been via direct mail; perhaps you had a team of people doing telesales or phone canvassing. These days you may have turned your attention to using Search Engine Optimisation (SEO) or Pay per Click (PPC) via a provider such as Google.

However, relying on a new method at the expense of old ones such as direct marketing or a system of referral can be as much of a mistake as living in the past and resisting the new e-marketing era altogether.

The percentage of business conducted online is increasing month on month, and many businesses now rely upon Internet marketing and monitoring methods to raise the profile of their business (see Further Resources for more information).

It is as important to monitor the effectiveness of your online marketing as it is every other kind of campaign, so that you can tell whether to repeat or adapt your methods in future. It is all too easy to spend a fortune on marketing without forward planning and without monitoring the response. For example, if you are spending money on Google Adwords to drive traffic to your website, first make sure you have set a budget and capped daily spend; second, monitor and measure the results.

You need to know:

- How many hits you get on your website.
- The conversion rate.
- How many people who visited your site contacted you or purchased something.

- What position you hold on the Google page.
- What your cost is 'per click'.
- How much it costs you to get people to visit your website.
- What keyword gives you the best conversion rate. (You may get 100 visitors with one keyword and ten visitors with another key word, but if you get more conversions from the lower group it may be worth spending more money on that particular keyword.)
- Google Analytics can provide you with reports to give you vital information, or your web company may be able to help. (Refer to a download on the Do It! or Ditch It website for more information on Google Adwords.)

Even free methods can be time-hungry. Monitor your marketing time and your budget so that you know definitively what has given you the greatest return. The Return on Investment (ROI) in terms of both time and money will drive your future decisions. If you have evidence you can evaluate it and use the Do It! or Ditch It decision-making tools:

- On a scale of 1 to 10, will this marketing activity take me closer to or further from my goal?
- Do I feel comfortable about taking this action? If I am feeling anxious, what further action do I need to take to decide whether this will be a safe, pioneering or unwise marketing activity?
- Will this campaign appeal to everyone?

There has never been a better time to network for free and make yourself visible online. But your profile needs to be planned in advance. Don't use social networking in a casual way. Everything you post online needs to send a consistent message about who you are and what you offer. If you want to be seen as a professional and you are charging appropriately for your services, it is worth investing in a professional website that reflects that professionalism. Remember that a poorly designed website will lose you business.

YOUR WEBSITE CHECKLIST

Ask yourself:

'What is the purpose of my website?'
'How will I drive people to my site?'
'Does the site contain key messages that reflect the values of my brand?'
'What do I want my visitors to do after visiting?'
'How will I capture and use the data?'
'What will visitors gain from my site?'
'Is there something I can give away free, to encourage registration?'
'Can I provide an interesting weekly or monthly blog?'
'Who can I link with to mutual benefit?'
*'Should I join a business networking site?' (If so, add a link to the
    home page.)*

TEST YOUR MARKET

One of the most common mistakes in business is to take action based on an assumption rather than on hard facts. This can be an expensive way of learning a hard lesson. For example, if you are planning a mailshot to 10,000 people using an untried mailing list, don't waste money by sending the information to all 10,000 people immediately. You don't yet know whether the list is of good quality. Instead, try 500 first, or perhaps split it in two and send a different mailshot to each group of 500. You may want to try two different approaches and two separate codes, too, and then monitor the response from each. I once used 500 with a professional message and 500 with a cartoon message and in that instance the cartoon generated more sales that the professional approach; but whatever you do, you *must* test and measure. Once you have monitored the response from the test mailing, *then* evaluate whether you want to mail the rest of the 10,000 names.

Give before you receive, to add value

Email marketing can bring fantastic results but, again, you must test the list before you purchase or rent email addresses. If a company won't agree to allow you to test 500 or 1,000 before purchasing, go elsewhere. I suggest you rent a list rather than buy one. Rather than trying to sell something, create an eBook, MP3, report, tips or other incentives as a free download. That way, when people enter their email address they get the benefit of a download and you have their email address for future emails. Everybody wins. Make sure you include an 'opt out' option, though, so that you don't send spam to people who don't want future mailings.

Evaluate your sale

It is important to monitor and measure the return on investment of everything you do. Do you know where your new prospects and your confirmed sales are coming from? Do you know whether they are likely to lead to new or repeat business? Where will your future sales come from? How can you create new leads?

Ask your customers and clients for feedback

Every decision you make will be related in some way to what your customers and clients want or need – so it makes sense to ask them for their feedback on how you are doing. It can be valuable to provide a brief questionnaire asking for client feedback, and give or send it to everyone you do business with and have done business with before. Don't censor the distribution: you will learn the most from those who have things to say that you may not want to hear. If you send one out every time you issue an invoice there will be an ongoing supply of feedback.

Ask yourself: are they scoring you as average? Great – that means you know that you can do better. Feedback means you know where you are – and what you need to do to monitor, measure and improve – on an ongoing basis.

DISCover HOW TO APPEAL TO A BROADER MARKET

Taking as an example a life coaching business, a useful exercise would be to step into each of the DISC styles.

Appealing to D-style customers

D-styles are 'bottom-line' focused so increase the level of results-orientated material you include. Keep images strong, powerful and energetic. What words are being used to imply winning and being the best? Is the message short and to the point?

- D-styles will want to get the message fast and will want to know that the product or service is the best there is.
- High D-styles tend to be impatient; they like instant results and fast delivery.
- D-styles will also make quick decisions for buying and generally don't seek the opinion of others.

Appealing to I-style customers

I-styles will want to know that they are valued customers or that the provider will welcome them. They enjoy being courted.

- High I-styles like social proof. Are any celebrities using the product or service?
- I-styles like interaction to be fun and friendly. They can be impulsive shoppers and like to buy from people they like.

Appealing to S-style customers

Use reassuring and caring language to appeal to this group. Money is a means to an end rather than the end in itself for this style, so a greater focus on people will get attention.

Does the campaign reassure the client or customer? Does it project a safe message? Are results guaranteed?

- S-styles will want to be reassured that their money is being well spent. They care about safety: for example, keeping children safe, choosing a safe car.
- S-styles will often want to ask opinions of friends and family before making a big purchase.

Appealing to C-style customers

C-styles will want the information to be presented in an ordered way that is easily accessible and accurate – and they will want plenty of it. Gratuitous images or unnecessary gimmicks will irritate this style.

Is the core message well validated? Are there any extreme claims that need to be toned down or backed up with data?

- C-styles will want to be reassured that the company is credible and that they are dealing with experts.
- C-styles are comparative shoppers and like to know they have the best deal.
- C-styles will do their research before making a significant purchase.

The DO IT! client finder

Knowing what you want is the best way to make sure it happens. This simple exercise is designed to help you to focus on what you want and need from your customer profile:

My ideal customer/ client would be:	My best customer/ client is:	Core characteristics

In the left column, 'My ideal customer/client would be', write down all the attributes of the people or organisations you would prefer to work with. Think only of what you want – not who your customer is – at this point.

Consider the following attributes. If you work with individuals as customers, their:

- Age
- Gender
- Education
- Profession
- Role/function
- Status
- Income
- Location
- Character

In the middle column, 'My best customer/client is', write down all the attributes your best customer has (good or bad). Visualise just one person who embodies your ideal customer, and capture as much detail as possible about that person. Imagine his/her day from morning to night. Write as much detail as possible, even going so far as to give that person a name, age, job, family structure (single, married, parent), work situation, recreational outlets and worries.

Circle any similarities in the two columns. For example, you may prefer to work with people who are a similar age to yourself and who are at managerial level, and your best customer may be at managerial level. There's a similarity.

Once you have finished circling, see if you notice a lot of similarities between the two columns. These become the right-hand column, 'Core characteristics', of your customer/client profile.

In defining your target audience and your niche market, you will find it an easier and more straightforward task to design a marketing strategy that will reach and develop your ideal target market. The more you give people what they want, the more often they will come back and the more you will enjoy working with them.

KNOW YOUR MARKET NICHE

Knowing where you sit in the marketplace alongside your competitors is very important. There is little point in launching a new idea or service unless you can be certain that you can equal or better the competition.

You will have created a SWOT analysis for your business plan (page 78). I always recommend repeating the SWOT process specifically from a marketing perspective, so that you can make sure that anything you spend is focused on reinforcing your strengths while transforming your weaknesses, opportunities and threats.

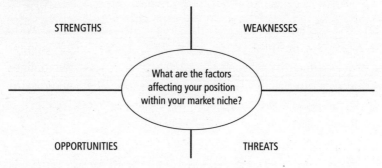

For example: business owner of a retail outlet for children's clothes in a small country town.

Strengths:	Product knowledge, high-quality goods, customer loyalty.
Weaknesses:	Too few local customers, low turnover, local population less than 10,000.
Opportunities:	Online sales, e-marketing, advertising, wholesale, PR.
Threats:	Lack of knowledge of e-marketing, high premises overheads, low turnover, no contacts in wholesale.

This business cannot compete effectively with others in their niche because the outlet is invisible to the majority of customers. Spending on traditional forms of marketing such as advertising may not significantly increase the customer base because the local population is so small. Display advertising has to be repeated at regular intervals to be effective. E-marketing is likely to deliver the greatest return on investment.

PENNY POWER'S GUIDE TO DEVELOPING A DIGITAL MINDSET

As the founder of business networking community Ecademy, Penny Power is a great believer in the benefits of social media. She recognised very early on that it is a fast and effective way to make new business connections and to make things happen – provided the quality controls are in place. She sees the online world as a way to create and enhance personal reputation, to attract your ideal 'followers'.

'I like to be "Open, Random and Supportive" (ORS) online,' says Penny, 'as I believe this is what people will respond to best. It is similar to being a friend. Those who are "Closed, Selective and Controlling" (CSC) are showing an old approach to business: targeted and in it only for themselves. Online communication is very much a two-way process. When you share your knowledge online, you are not seeking sales, you want to become better known. It is about showing your value to others so that you receive back from them in ways that will benefit your business in the longer term. Social media is not a replacement for human contact. I hate to be tied to a PC, as do most people. But if you start to create daily habits that keep your online presence fresh, relevant and useful to others, the benefits will be significant. Make sure you set up the technology so it is easy to do and then do it through a Smartphone while you are on the move.'

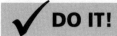 **DO IT!**

MARKETING ACTION POINTS

- Address lack of knowledge of e-marketing by reading or getting trained up on the subject.
- Build relationships with local journalists to try to secure PR in the form of a personal story about the business.
- Create a marketing plan.
- Don't restrict yourself to using only one or two marketing media; use several. Become an expert marketer, or hire one to help you.
- Stay true to your company values.

COMPANY VALUES

Many businesses stand for something bigger than their company. Decisions around to what extent your values drive your ethos are both personally and economically driven.

Corporations that are involved in charitable concerns or have incorporated environmental issues within their corporate ethos tend to have a greater level of loyalty among their customers.

- Timberland commit to planting a quota of trees each year.
- Sawdays are having an impact on people's holiday and leisure choices – by making organic and green issues integral to the selection criteria for their holiday homes.
- The Fairtrade and Soil Association marks are quality assurances that show purchasers that contributing companies have made value-based decisions about their trading practices.

BUILD A BUSINESS NETWORK

Your business is only as strong as your client or customer base. Your customer network is crucial to your long-term survival. When you are respected in your industry people will recommend you, doors will open without you having to knock on them and business will become much easier.

There is a saying that goes, 'A friend is simply a stranger who you haven't met yet.' This has never been truer than in the current age of Internet marketing. Social networking sites such as Facebook, LinkedIn, Twitter and many others have created new sales routes for many savvy companies. Not everything in business needs a price tag. There are times when doing someone a favour may pay dividends in the longer term. So:

- Be tolerant.
- Strive to be a person with integrity; invest in relationships.
- Be a person who is admired and is good to be around.
- Don't moan or groan. Everyone in business has challenges.
- Help others to help you by knowing what you want and brief clearly.
- Pay or supply promptly.

The role of marketing is to turn needs into wants and to convert new customers to your brand. When you begin, your customers are strangers. You believe they will like you, once they get to know you, but first they need to know you are there and learn to understand and trust you. Building a customer base from scratch can take months or even years.

- ***Future business.*** Deciding how to find new business can be expensive. It is important to weigh up in advance what the likely return is going to be before spending any money.

- **Prospects.** New prospects may not have bought anything from you yet, but they have agreed to let you market to them by joining your mailing list. What do you know about them? How can you turn their curiosity into a true need or want?
- **Current customers.** These are the people who have bought from you this year. (If it has been longer than that, they become prospects again.) What else can you sell to them? It is easier to sell to existing customers than to find new ones.
- **Repeat business.** These are your most valued customers. They will buy from you again and again. They sing your praises to others and give you word-of-mouth endorsements. Look after them.

It is wise to develop the discipline of ensuring that every marketing decision is made in the context of a marketing plan, and a marketing budget has been allocated to support that plan. Visit www.BevJames.com for a wealth of free business downloads, planning templates and other resources.

Your marketing plan maps, monitors and measures the following:

- The USP for your product or service.
- The price or scale of charges.
- The discount structure (if there is one).
- Who you are targeting.
- Who is buying.
- What they are buying – and what else they might buy.
- The demographic: how many people and what kind of people?
- Supply: from receipt of order to delivery of goods.
- Distribution: storage, transportation.
- Promotion: plans for promoting the product.

Your sales strategy will ask:

- Who will sell your product or service?
- Who will they sell to?
- How will they sell?
- What will they sell?
- What are their targets?
- The price or scale of charges.
- The discount structure (if there is one).

BUILD A CUSTOMER PROFILE

How much do you know about the characteristics that connect all of those people who want your goods or services? Are you getting the kinds of customers and clients that you want – or that you need? What is your market niche?

I always advise people to set their sights on working with those clients who bring out the best in them. If you can relate to the needs, wants, problems and challenges of those who come to you for your products or services, you are more likely to do a good job of helping them. (One of my own requirements is always to make sure I am working with people who have a Do It! mindset and are and positive in their outlook.) You are much more likely to shine if you are enjoying what you do and feel a sense of connection with your clients.

IS BUSINESS BAD? OR ARE YOU BAD AT PITCHING?

One of the biggest mistakes a service company can make is to be so focused on their own profile and what they have to offer that they forget to consider *what the customer really wants and needs*.

I recently had a need for three different office services for my business. I contacted and met with six suppliers to find out more information and to get some quotes. Not one of them convinced me that they had what it takes to deliver what I needed. Here are some of the mistakes they made:

- Didn't call me back or answer email fast enough.
- Came to the meeting without having done any research on my company.
- Made no effort to build a rapport before jumping into the detail. (This needs to be assessed depending on whether your prospective client seems more people- or task-orientated.)
- Set up a long and boring PowerPoint presentation with company history.
- Made no attempt to close the sale or arrange to follow up.
- Did not follow up after the meeting.

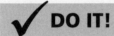 **DO IT!**

SEVEN ESSENTIALS TO HELP YOUR CUSTOMER DECIDE TO USE YOUR SERVICES

1. Reply to enquiries on the same day you receive them if you don't want to miss out on the opportunity.
2. Do your research on your customer, so that you have a sense of their needs before you get to the meeting.
3. Keep your presentation brief and relevant (and avoid 'death by PowerPoint').
4. Ask questions. Spend time finding our exactly what your customer wants, and aim to fill that need. What problem are you helping to solve and what difference will it make to them?
5. Ask what you need to do to get the order.
6. Summarise the requirements to make sure you have understood the needs correctly.
7. Close the deal or arrange follow-up.

DO IT! OR DITCH IT CHECKLIST

HOW?

Sales and marketing

How are you approaching your sales and marketing plans? Have you identified your market niche? Do you know your typical customer profile? Your level of clarity will help you to assess whether you have done all you need to ensure you have enough customers and clients to make your business viable.

Try using the simple scale that follows to assess your current state of readiness. Consider each characteristic below and rate by marking where on the line your state of mind lies. Do you feel closer to the right-hand column, or the left-hand column?

This exercise does not evaluate the strategy itself. There are no 'good feelings' or 'bad feelings' and no rights or wrongs. It is a way to assess your frame of mind. On balance, are you in a 'Do It!' frame of mind? Or is that critical voice inside your head suggesting you should 'Ditch It' because you don't have a clear sales strategy?

CHECK YOUR MINDSET

On a scale of 1 to 10, how close are you to your goal?

1 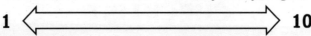 **10**

The 'Ditch It' Warning Signs	The 'Do It!' Mindset
We want to appeal to everyone	I know our customer profile
I know what price the market can take	Our pricing policy is based on a clear profit margin that includes all costs
The lease is going cheaply	We are in an ideal location
Everyone will buy it	Our initial forecasts are modest
My product will sell itself	We have an aggressive sales strategy
Advertising should work	We are doing a lot of marketing for free
There are 1,000 names on the database	We are testing several mailing lists already
All we need is our website	Our website is attracting registration
I will need to learn on the job	I have previous experience in this area
It is very hard to quantify marketing activity	Every activity will be monitored and measured

WHAT ACTIONS WILL TAKE YOU ONE STEP CLOSER TO YOUR GOAL?

WRITE THEM HERE

STEP 6: HOW MUCH?

Is the concept profitable?

FINANCIAL MANAGEMENT

'Business must be run at a profit, else it will die.
But when anyone tries to run a business solely for profit ...
then also the business must die, for it no longer
has a reason for existence.'

Henry Ford

Step 6: HOW MUCH? The financial element is crucial to your business. Fine-tune your DISC traits for finance. Set long-term financial goals and short-term controls. Make sure your business plan is built on solid financial foundations. Plan for profit, account for overheads, control costs, understand finance.

Beware the danger zone: some people have a greater capacity for financial detail than others, but even if management accounts don't fire you up with as much enthusiasm as other topics, it is still important to stay on top of money matters and to know the facts and figures inside out. I always know exactly how much my businesses have in the bank and exactly how much we are invoicing on a monthly basis; I know exactly what our outgoings are and I approve all expenditure, large and small. Keeping your finger on the financial pulse is essential. *Ditch* any deals that aren't working for you and *Do* make sure you are making more than you spend. Keeping in control of your costs is key to keeping your business.

Step 6 is all about finance. It considers the Do It! or Ditch It decisions that need to be made during the evaluation stages of running a business, and the management decisions that influence daily cash flow and long-term profit. The content in this chapter is vital for decision-making success. Every business person, whether they are launching a new idea, have been in business for several years or are planning a major business expansion, needs to keep their finances under control. A business is not a hobby – it is a commercial venture that has to keep profitability to the fore at all times. Whether you are working in the business or own the business, you are responsible for safeguarding cash flow and profits. No matter who you approach for investment sign-off or business advice, you are the one who is responsible for the commercial success or failure of your idea.

At the most basic level, it makes sense to: do more of those things that make a profit, ditch those things that make a loss. Of course, it is not always as simple as that, because from a marketing perspective there are occasions when it makes sense to give something away for free in order to gain in the longer term; or occasions when taking less profit provides greater value to the company in some other way. However, when focusing on finance, it pays to keep things simple. In order for your company to succeed you need more money to be coming in than you are paying out; and your cash flow needs to be tightly managed at all times.

HOW MUCH RISK?

Are you a sole trader, set up as a limited company or operating as a business partnership? Each business model has its strengths and weaknesses and if you are unsure what is best for you, ask the advice of your accountant or use a credible online resource to research your options.

It makes sense to ensure that you can manage your outgoings before you set up in business. If you are carrying a large amount of debt from a previous venture or your overheads are high, you may need to take financial advice before you embark on a new project. No matter how brilliant you feel your new idea to be, starting from a position of negative equity is never a comfortable one.

There is more than one way to make money from an idea. If you are not in a position to set up yourself, look at selling the concept to a third party and building up your capital reserves in that way. Few true entrepreneurs are 'one-hit wonders': most will have another idea up their sleeves before too long.

> Remember: if you operate as a sole trader, your personal overheads will have as much impact on the bottom line of your company as business overheads. If one of your clients is slow to pay, your home as well as your business may be at risk.

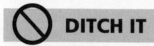 **DITCH IT**

TEN SIGNS THAT YOUR BRILLIANT IDEA MAY BE A BUSINESS RISK

1. You are over-optimistic. Your market research is based solely on your own enthusiasm for the product or service.
2. Your business plan and costings are based on supposition rather than verifiable facts.
3. You have not prepared a cash-flow projection for the year ahead.
4. You are a sole trader and your personal costs are greater than your projected earnings.
5. You can't read a profit and loss account.
6. You are not motivated by the idea of making a profit.
7. You don't enjoy sales or marketing.

8. You do not have the means to deliver what you are promising your customers.

9. You have sunk a lot of capital into new stock that will need to be stored, without a clear idea of how to sell it.

10. Your accountant tells you that the figures don't add up.

Newspapers and get-rich-quick books are full of stories that talk about high-risk ventures that have succeeded and millionaires who have apparently made their money by 'risking it all' on an 'overnight success'. The reality is usually far more mundane. Millions are made by those who are financially alert and can recognise opportunities rather than those who are reckless or impulsive; by those who are enthusiastic about the business of business rather than emotionally attached to the idea itself. If your heart is ruling your head – BEWARE. There is a time for caution as well as drive in business – and that often surrounds the matter of financial planning.

GILL FIELDING'S ADVICE FOR SETTING UP IN BUSINESS

Gill Fielding is co-owner of the Wealth Company and many others. She made her first million through property. In her teens and twenties she had several jobs at once and after saving hard she bought her first property in 1977 at the age of 19. It cost £7,500. Three years later she sold it for four times that amount. Since then she has bought and sold many businesses and it is now her mission to help others to make money.

> 'Property prices were on a steep rise and it was a golden time for investment. I just kept reinvesting my profits in new properties and kept my wits about me. My approach has always been to look to the long term with my investments. Prudence is very important to me. I am quite cautious with money.'

 **DO IT!**

GILL'S TOP TIPS FOR SOUND FINANCIAL DECISION-MAKING ARE:

1. *Test your market cheaply. Focus initially on selling one of your products or services to one complete stranger. If you can manage that, then you can sell more. Do this before you spend too much money on infrastructure or things like business cards.*

2. *Use other people's expertise: ask for help, share ideas and joint venture. I've always thought that 50 per cent of something is better than 100 per cent of nothing and have always shared profits. Make sure you concentrate on what you CAN do rather than what you can't.*

3. *A dynamic small business can outwit a larger business in the same market every time – but will have fewer resources. Be 'fast, focused, flexible and friendly'.*

4. *Remember that turnover is great, profit is better, but CASH is the ideal. You must always manage the cash flow FIRST as lack of cash will eventually shut you down.'*

DISCover YOUR ATTITUDE TO FINANCE

Financial management is a discipline that can be adopted by anyone, whatever their primary DISC characteristics. However, the attitude to finance income, expenditure, controls and Key Performance Indicators (KPIs) may vary.

The D-style

Often the risk taker, the D-style will more often than not adopt an aggressive approach to situations, particularly challenging ones. If their business needs to compete, they may well run an aggressive campaign and push the boundaries of the marketing budget. If cost savings need to be made by 'releasing' personnel, they will do so, generally without emotional attachment.

The D-style generally likes financial information to be brief and to the point, preferably with a bullet-point summary at the end. D-styles like to be made aware when additional information can help them achieve their success – or they may endanger its provision.

- The challenge for the D-style is to wait until enough information has been collated before taking action.

The I-style

Ever the optimist, more often than not the I-style will respond to challenges by adopting persuasive tactics. If their business needs to compete, they may well launch a sales and marketing campaign with little or no regard for cost, because their optimism will tell them that it will work. If it does not work, they will probably throw some more money at it, even if the budget is spent.

The I-style can have a 'Don't worry, it will all be OK' approach, because they often feel that they can make enough sales eventually. The I-style's challenge is to focus on costs. They may need to ask someone to prepare a brief summary report in order to know where the business is on a daily basis, or develop the discipline of dealing with costs on a daily basis. If cuts need to be made, the I-style will often have difficulty letting people go because of their fear of losing popularity.

- The challenge for the I-style is to remain realistic about their financial situation.

The S-style

With their focus on safety, the S-style is looking primarily for business sustainability. The safety-conscious S-style will want to evaluate the risks regarding costs before deciding to take action. If their business needs to compete, the S-style will often take a passive approach and will probably not want to put all their eggs in one basket, electing instead to hold something back in reserve. The S-style will prefer to think ahead regarding costs and cost controls and avoid the need to make cuts; however, should the need arise, they would seek options elsewhere rather than lose personnel in the first instance.

- The challenge for the S-style is to take a calculated risk now and then.

The C-style
The C-style prefers an ordered approach to financial management and will generally want to stick to the rules. In the case of finance, the rules are the *agreed* figures on the budget. The C-style may refer people to the fact that the figures down on paper are there by the agreement of all; if no one is going to abide by them, what is the point of committing them to paper in the first place?

If their business needs to compete, the C-style will try to do it within the budget or save money elsewhere in order to release funds. The C-style does not like to overspend – unless they can see that it has generated or is likely to generate more income. Many C-styles, however, manage costs at the expense of generating more income year on year, which can result in lack of business growth.

If cuts need to be made, C-styles generally have a plan in the background *just in case* and will take what they perceive to be the most logical action.

- The challenge for the C-style is quite often to become less risk-averse.

MANAGING PROFITABLITY

Remember that profit is sales minus costs.

That means *all* costs.

It is essential that you have fully worked out the total cost of running your business before taking the plunge. You will need to identify both fixed and variable costs.

Fixed costs: These are costs that remain the same whether you make zero sales or one hundred.

For example:

- Rent
- Rates
- Salaries
- Accountancy costs

Variable costs: These are normally linked to a percentage of sales. So, if you make more than one sale these costs would change.

For example:

- Raw materials
- The cost of manufacturing
- Commissions
- Online bank charges (per sale)
- Delivery costs

A certain level of fixed cost will be inevitable at the start-up stage of running a business and there may be a delay of a few weeks or months before that cost can be recovered. A common weak spot for new businesses is an unrealistic expectation of how quickly revenue can be earned back to cover the cost of start-up. This may result in buying too much stock, taking on too many staff or adopting a price policy that is based on volume sales rather than adopting a more cautious approach to forecasting.

If your business model is very simple it may be possible to lump all costs together and allocate them on a pro rata basis to the unit cost of the goods you are selling. This can be a useful rule of thumb when assessing how the business is doing on a daily basis, but is inappropriate for management accounting purposes.

Points to consider when planning for profitability

- How much capital will the company need during the set-up stage?
- How much working capital will be required once the business is up and running?
- Can you put an accurate figure on your costs?
- How much will the goods or services cost to produce (design, manufacture, distribute, market, sell, store)?
- How much profit will the goods or services make per unit, hour, day, week, month, year?
- How will the business charge its products or services?
- How will the company collect revenues?
- What will your trading terms and conditions be?
- What cash controls will be required?
- What is your breakeven?

Breaking even

Breakeven occurs at the point where your sales have generated enough revenue to cover both the fixed costs and the variable costs of the sales made.

Achieving breakeven is the minimum essential if your business is to remain viable.

Cash

Once you have worked through your numbers and decided that your business will be profitable, you need to ensure you have enough cash to generate the profit. The ultimate aim is a cash-positive business.

The cash-positive business

This means you get paid for your goods or services *before* you pay out cash for buying them. If your business operates in this way, the amount of cash required will be low.

The cash-negative business

This means you pay for goods first and then sell them to get income. These businesses are generally services where an invoice is issued and the recipient may take sixty days to pay. This means a company may well spend more than it receives during a set period of time, typically often over a quarter, which is a dangerous cash situation to be in.

 **DO IT!**

WAYS TO TURN CASH NEGATIVE INTO CASH POSITIVE

Can you turn your cash-negative business into a cash-positive one? If you reach the conclusion that your business is cash negative and your business is at risk because it is under-capitalised (with not enough cash to spend), there are some options available to you.

Request payment in advance

Advance or phased payments are the most obvious but often the most overlooked option – this will immediately change your business from negative to positive. However, you will need to know your market/customers/competition as this course of action may well have an adverse effect on the business relationship – unless it is the industry norm.

Request deposits with order
If payment in advance is not an option, a deposit with the order will certainly be the next best option.

Offer your customers a small discount for early payment
Simple yet effective – you will need to ensure the discount level is correct because you don't want it to have an adverse effect on your overall profit.

Invoice factoring
Invoice factoring (through a factoring company) enables you to get paid when you raise your invoices, regardless of when your customer actually pays you. It takes away all the difficulties of chasing money and helps removes the worry of not knowing when you might get paid. Instead of waiting for customers to pay your invoices, after goods are delivered you send copies of your customers' invoices to the factoring company and then draw up to 90 per cent of the value immediately. The factoring company will charge for this service.

Invoice discounting
Invoice discounting is a loan that is made to a business by a bank or another financial institution. The loan is secured against the value of outstanding invoices (money owed to the business, by its customers).

Buy from a UK supplier, not overseas
Though cost might be higher, it will reduce lead times and give you more chance of getting trade credit.

Negotiate better terms with your suppliers

If you don't ask, you definitely will not get. All they can say is 'No' – and they may well say Yes'!

 DITCH IT

- If you can see that you will always be struggling for cash and cannot change the business model – ditching your business may be the only answer.

HOW TO NEGOTIATE

The business of business is business – and the profit always lies at the point of negotiation. This applies to everything from the day-to-day purchasing of office stationery, to the terms of the lease when renting office space, to your terms of business when selling to your customers. My own business mentor, Peter Thomson, offers the following tips on how to negotiate effectively. He taught me never to be embarrassed to ask for a discount.

Peter's methods saved me over £2,000 when I was getting my house redesigned. When the builder's merchants gave me their price I learned to say: 'And what is that after you have given me a discount?' Even in a situation where a discount on the goods is not achievable, you may gain another benefit instead. In one negotiation I achieved free delivery that would otherwise have cost me £120.

I have since learned to apply this strategy to my business negotiations, too. When first I took over The Coaching Academy I renegotiated with every supplier, which saved the company tens of thousands of pounds in the first year.

- **Speak to the decision-maker.** There's no point in getting into an in-depth discussion with someone who is not authorised to make a decision because the situation will be stressful for them and non-productive for you. If you are looking the person in the eye it becomes harder for them to say, 'Yes, I have the authority, but no, you're not having a discount'. Peter Thomson has a great line: 'Are you authorised to give discount?' If someone says "Yes" then that suggests that a discount could be available. If they say "No", ask who is authorised and ask to speak to them. When they appear, say, "I hear you are authorised to give a discount". They will often say "Yes" with pride – so off you go ...

- **Don't take things at face value.** If you buy or take over an existing business that has been having cash-flow problems, don't be shy about renegotiating your suppliers' terms of contract. It can be a life-saving strategy for the business.

- **Adopt the negotiation habit.** Practise makes perfect in negotiation. Make negotiation a part of every acquisition you make. If people say 'No' it really doesn't matter. At least you have tried.

- **Don't get embarrassed.** Many of us, particularly in Western society, are brought up to accept prices at face value; we feel embarrassed to question what is on the label. But survival in business is about making a profit, so if you get used to negotiating, you will become better at making money.

- **It's not personal.** When you ask, 'Is that your best price?' 'Is there anything you can do for me on the price?' it is not a personal attack or a judgement. They are just phrases that another business person will understand.

CASH AND WORKING CAPITAL

Cash is the lifeblood of any business. Without it, sudden death can become a distinct possibility. Inefficient cash management remains the primary cause of business failure. So what are the secrets of managing cash flow? What should you DO more often and which practices should you DITCH?

Every invoice or payment made follows a cycle, known as the operating cycle:

Outgoing cash: goods bought, invoice received, invoice paid.

Incoming cash: goods sold, invoice generated, payment received.

Problems occur when the amount of money due to be paid to suppliers is higher than the incoming cash due.

For example: an aromatherapist buys essential oils for her soap-making business and pays fifteen days after delivery. On average it takes thirty days to sell the soap and then another five for the credit card companies to deposit customers' money into the company bank account.

Therefore the operating cycle is 30 + 5 − 15 = 20 days.

This means that the business pays its suppliers twenty days before receiving cash from customers. To cover this cost an overdraft arrangement will probably need to be in place.

A danger point can occur within a business that is expanding rapidly, because the level of outgoings increases faster than the rate of sale and speed of the cash coming in, even if the product margins are good. This is known as *over-trading.*

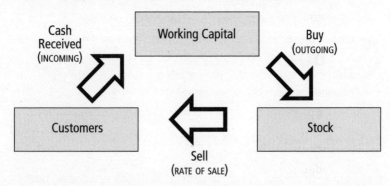

The most effective way to manage this process is to devise an appropriate cash-flow system so that you keep close track of your working capital. Include every element of your business and list, on a monthly basis:

- Cash out
- Cash in
- The difference:
1. How big is the difference in monetary value?
2. If it is a negative balance, where will the money come from?
3. Looking forward, reduce this cash-flow risk by using the negative to positive steps (above)

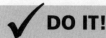 DO IT!

- Aim to remain cash positive at all times.
- Invoice promptly.
- Negotiate extended payment terms with your suppliers.
- Consider offering a discount for payment on delivery.
- Consider making large payments, for example your payroll, on a monthly rather than a weekly basis.
- Understand more about your customers' buying cycle.
- Adopt a 'just in time' approach to buying supplies or stock.
- Pay cheques and cash into your bank account promptly.
- Renegotiate the terms of your overdraft with your bank.

DITCH IT

- Over-producing or over-purchasing stock.
- Offering product or business services that are not financially productive.
- Poor cash management.
- Bad creditors.
- Extended credit terms.
- Unnecessary overheads.

JAMIE CONSTABLE'S GUIDE TO MANAGING CASH FLOW

As a venture capitalist, Jamie Constable knows that cash management is critical. 'You've got to get your invoice out as quickly as you possibly can. No matter how small you are, a cash management system is essential, with someone in place to collect the money that is due. Ask yourself how you can make your client or customer pay you before you have to pay anybody else.

Make sure that you:

- *Collect cash quickly.*
- *Don't pay cash out too quickly.*
- *Supply clear terms and conditions in advance.*
- *Stay in regular contact with customers and suppliers.*
- *Let people know about billing in advance.*
- *Offer discount incentives for fast payment.*
- *Renegotiate terms with your suppliers, regularly.*

A successful business needs to make a cash profit as quickly as possible, and making sure your margins are right is fundamental to success. It is generally much easier to make more from your existing customers than to try to win new customers.

Ask yourself:

- *How can we make more out of our existing customers?*
- *How can we make the agreement more cash efficient?*
- *What else can we sell them?*
- *How can we improve the profit margin?*
- *Can we get payment up front?*

It's better to walk away if you think there is a financial risk, no matter how good you think the opportunity is.'

WATCH YOUR OVERHEADS

Many people who start up in business for the first time have a preconceived idea that they need to form a limited company and will need premises, but there are other options. Setting up as a sole trader and operating from home, sub-leasing within someone else's space or even running a market stall can all be cheaper ways of getting your business off the ground initially. Keeping overheads to a minimum should always be the prime objective when first starting up. I get very nervous when new business owners talk more about spending money than they do about how they are going to make it.

An office of your own may seem like a lovely idea, but is the lease more than your business can afford at this stage? Resist committing to spending too much on overheads before you are certain of what your business is going to earn. Premises are not always essential. In fact, a strong online presence may be much more effective. Over 500,000 people start up their own business every year – and of the 4.8 million businesses currently operating in the UK, over 2 million are run from home. A further 7.5 million people run their business from home.

If offices or retail space is a must, consider leasing serviced office space in a buoyant area to test whether that is the ideal location from which to grow the business. (But make sure their terms are flexible.) Once you are confident that your business is in profit and you have definitely chosen the right location, you can take the actions necessary to make more permanent arrangements.

Lease warning

Many landlords seek personal financial guarantees on leases – I would strongly advise that you avoid this scenario because, if you sign a fifteen-year lease and give a personal guarantee, this means that you personally (not your company) will guarantee the rental payment on that property for fifteen years – regardless of whether your business occupies the premises or not. For example:

• You give a personal financial guarantee on a fifteen-year lease.
• After five years you sell the business.
• Two years later the people you sold to go bust.
• The business is not let to another person.
• You are now liable for the rent going forward – in this case eight years.
• You are also liable for any unpaid rent by the previous tenants.

Always seek independent legal advice before entering into any type of lease agreement. The danger can often be your initial enthusiasm and positive outlook that the business will work, so always look at the downside, too. As Matt Dyer (see page 136) testifies, this one piece of information saved him a considerable amount of money.

'When I worked for Bev nearly twenty years ago, she gave me a very crucial piece of advice, which was, 'Don't put down personal financial guarantees for anything'. That advice, more recently, possibly saved my business. My company had taken out a lease on a building that, unbeknown to me, was a frequent target for break-ins. We were burgled six times. I wasn't locked into the lease, because I had listened to the advice that I had been given – and so I was able to relocate. The strategy probably saved my business. The moral for me is to listen to everyone around you and to absorb as much information as you can, because you never know when it will be useful.'

SEEKING INVESTMENT

Many businesses need investment finance in order to achieve their goals. Whether this comes in the form of a short-term overdraft or a long-term loan will depend on the nature of the business and the scale of the owner's ambitions. Business dragon James Caan often says that the first £100–£250,000 that you need to raise for your business or idea is probably the hardest amount of money you will ever need to raise, because your business idea may be untried; you have no track record; you may have very little collateral to support your loan requirements.

Typically an investor will want to see the following documentation:

- A business plan for the next few years showing growth in revenue, cash and profit.
- History of the business.
- Details of management experience.
- Details of the market, products, existing customer base and suppliers.
- Details of major competitors or substitute products.
- Details of any Intellectual Property protection.
- Historic balance sheet, profit and loss and cash-flow statements.
- Recent management accounts.
- Detailed forecasts of operating performance and cash flow over two to five years.
- For lenders, details of owners personal assets and wealth.
- Details of existing financing facilities.

Generally speaking, it is easier to borrow a very large sum of money than a small sum, because the opportunity for the investor to make a profit is that much larger scale. Finance in the form of OPM (other people's money) will usually come from one of five kinds of lender.

- **Banks.** For most businesses, the first port of call for borrowing will be a bank. Banks will usually lend money, even in times of recession, provided the borrower can offer some form of collateral or security. DO read the small print and make sure that the terms of repayment will not disadvantage you at a key stage in your early business development. DITCH any loan that has terms that are disadvantageous to the running of your business.

- **Friends and family.** Many people will turn initially to friends or family to borrow money because those who have belief in your idea and know you personally may be more likely to offer financial support without security. However, this can be a high-risk strategy for the lender. As a business owner DO borrow responsibly and DITCH the possibility of putting someone else's livelihood at short- or long-term risk in favour of your own gain.

- **Business angels.** The business angel network consists of organisations and groups of investors who club together to back promising new entrepreneurs. They tend to invest on a scale lower than £75,000 and can be an excellent source of support and funding. BBC TV's *Dragons' Den* shows the kind of benefits that are to be gained from business angels. DO seek the support of business angels, especially those who have had previous experience in your area of business. DITCH the expectation that you will retain autonomous control over your company.

- **Venture capitalists.** This group of investors will want a greater level of involvement in your business than any of the others. They are likely to attend monthly board meetings and will want access to reports that enable them to see how their investment is doing. DO be fully prepared before you pitch to an investor and remember that they can ask for their money and their profits back at any time. They will usually be expecting to make a profit over a period of three to five years and will either want their return as a dividend, or by selling their shares to a third party.

- **Private equity investors.** Similar to venture capitalists, private equity investors tend to focus on investing in experienced businesses.

Whatever the source of your borrowing, make sure you check the small print in the business deal and safeguard your home and your family from undue risk.

BUDGETING AND FORECASTING

When you go to investors or a bank to get funding, you will need to show a forecast of how the business is going to grow and how much finance you will require. A good forecast will show the benefit of the loan and whether you can afford it.

Your annual budget

This is a valuable benchmark that shows not only how your business has performed to date but also provides a benchmark to compare it to in the future. There are many ways to forecast, but the following questions should always be at the centre of your analysis:

- How much more can you sell next year?
- Will you have to increase or lower your prices?
- Do you need more staff, or a bigger office?
- What sort of infrastructure and staffing will you need?
- What is happening to your product cost or to your wage bill?

Operating costs

These will usually increase slightly each year if there are no major changes planned.

- Will you increase your fixed cost base?
- Have you taken account of an increase in your suppliers' prices?

- Will you make changes to the service or product?
- *Interest rates* and *exchange rates* will change, too, so you will need to factor in the changes.

Time frame

While almost all businesses forecast a year or more in advance, the truth is that in a volatile market they can often be out of date soon after they have been completed. This means you should be prepared to update your forecast to reflect changes in the market.

Detail

Break your forecast into manageable periods. If your business runs on a monthly cycle, then divide it monthly. Build in seasonal variations as well, and take account of the need for extra staff during busy periods.

JAMES CAAN'S GUIDE TO THE PERFECT PITCH

'In my view the perfect pitch should rarely be any longer than three minutes. Within that time you've got to be able to present your case, without going into every detail. Treat the opportunity like presenting your executive summary. You are trying to engage the interest of the potential investor, and take on your business journey.

It is wise to demonstrate the viability of the plan over a three-to-five-year period because that is the optimum length of time an investor will usually consider when wanting a return on that investment. Profits are unlikely in year one, so you've got to have a plan that's long enough to demonstrate what the return to the investor is.

The document is not the key influence. That lies in the ability to present and communicate the information in a manner that inspires the investor. It is the passion, the drive, the determination and the ability of the entrepreneur to execute the plan that will tell an investor whether someone has the unique ability to execute their idea.

Give the investor the opportunity to ask questions. You want them to say, "That really sounds quite interesting – how does it work?" "What are the margins?" Then you can use PowerPoint to interact and demonstrate you know what you're doing. Graphs, charts and so on are a useful way to present the facts and make them credible.

What not to do
Beware of causing "death by PowerPoint". The last thing an investor wants to hear is "Let me take you through the presentation", followed by twenty-five slides that take twenty minutes to show. You will rarely retain interest for that period of time.

Know your own value
Your personal saleability is very important. The plan's great, the numbers are great, the idea's great. But the question the investor wants answered is "Why you?" What is it about you that is going to make the big difference?

Explain your motivation
Take the investor through your journey – how have you got to this point? Why is this idea important to you? What sacrifices are you prepared to make to demonstrate to me that you will go the extra mile and make this happen? What's your commitment to this idea, and what have you put in so far?

I believe that it is the entrepreneur who is going to breathe life into the concept and idea. The entrepreneur is the fundamental component who may or may not make the idea fly. Personal commitment inspires confidence that you will protect the investment and not lose someone his money.

Someone who has a business concept should also be bringing substantial value to that idea through their contacts base, their relationships, understanding, drive and commercialism. All of those things are what build the idea. If the entrepreneur implies that they have nothing of personal value to add, it suggests that anyone can go off and do it. If anyone can do it, then an investor is not going to be interested. They want to know that the entrepreneur has something unique to offer. So I am always interested in investing in the person as well as the idea.

I never worry unduly about sharing my business ideas, because even if you take steps to protect your concept, you can't stop people copying. I've seen so many instances where, with just a small twist or change, someone else's idea is turned into a new proposition by a competitor, and they get round a patent.

You're always going to get competition, and people will always try to emulate what you do. That's just the nature of business. The advantage of being the first to market is that you can make a far greater impact than anyone who follows in your wake. A trail-blazer needs the personal drive to keep ahead of the pack. If you show belief in your potential for success, an investor is more likely to believe in you too.'

 **DO IT!**

TEN SIGNS THAT YOUR BUSINESS CONCEPT IS FINANCIALLY VIABLE

- Your business plan is realistic and looks modestly profitable from the outset.
- Your budget is realistic and based on known market factors.

- You already have enough advance orders to underwrite the cost of your time or production.
- You have done a test run and the production costs are realistic.
- Market trends suggest that there is an increasing requirement for your product or service.
- You have proven business experience in the industry and understand the product.
- You have tested the concept on industry contacts and they are enthusiastic about its potential.
- You have negotiated prompt payment by customers and longer payment terms with suppliers.
- You have quality controls in place.
- Your accountant is happy.

Money management is rarely much fun to read about but can be extremely exciting to monitor when the business is doing well. Develop strong financial management habits and use your accountant well and wisely, and you will greatly increase your chances of running a business profitably in an enduring fashion. Step 7: WHEN? looks further at financial management by managing and measuring business performance.

For more detailed explanation of financial terminology see pages 271-274

 **DO IT!**

PAUL RAGAN SAYS 'PLAN YOUR EXIT STRATEGY'

Channel 4's *The Secret Millionaire*'s Paul Ragan founded the cold-start insurance brokerage Motaquote in Cardiff at the age of just 23, having left school with few qualifications. He grew it into a multimillion-pound business and became Wales's youngest multimillionaire.

Plan your exit strategy

'The day you plan your exit strategy should be the day you start your business. It's important that all key players are agreed concerning what you are looking to achieve and that you focus on things that add maximum value to the business rather than just doing the things you want to do. That helps with day-to-day decision-making, too, and means that as a business owner you are making long-term decisions that keep the return on investment in mind.'

DO IT! OR DITCH IT CHECKLIST

HOW MUCH?

Financial management

How much attention are you paying to your finances? Cash flow is king in business.

Try using the simple scale that follows to assess your attitude to finance. Consider each characteristic below and rate by marking where on the line your state of mind lies. Do you feel closer to the right-hand column, or the left-hand column?

This exercise does not evaluate the state of your finances. There are no 'good feelings' or 'bad feelings' and no rights or wrongs. It is a way to assess your frame of mind.

On balance, are you in a 'Do It!' frame of mind? Or is that critical voice inside your head suggesting you should 'Ditch It' because the figures don't add up?

CHECK YOUR MINDSET

On a scale of 1 to 10, how close are you to your goal?

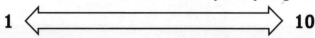

1   10

The 'Ditch It' Warning Signs

I leave the numbers to my accountant

The invoice follows when I have time

Our clients are slow payers

We don't care where the money comes from!

I don't negotiate

I just want to get started

We are always short of cash

We don't need a budget

I see my accountant once a year

It's not about money at the end of the day

The 'Do It!' Mindset

We have a system for cash-flow projection

We invoice promptly

We ask for cash up front

We don't want to put all our eggs in one basket

I am comfortable negotiating

I always provide a written quote

Cash in is higher than payment out

We have a budget and set targets

I talk to my accountant regularly

Cash is king

WHAT ACTIONS WILL TAKE YOU ONE STEP CLOSER TO YOUR GOAL?

WRITE THEM HERE

STEP 7: WHEN?

When will you see results?

MANAGING YOUR BUSINESS

'Think like a customer, act like a business manager.'

Step 7: WHEN? focuses on management decision-making. The ongoing process of daily prioritisation is where the true success of a business takes place. After all the excitement of big-picture planning, the task of maintaining enthusiasm for the daily detail and the smaller decisions can be challenging.

The Do It! approach to business decisions means planning ahead – while keeping your eye on the end goal. Sailors and pilots know that if they are one degree off course when planning their route, they can end up hundreds of miles from where they intended to land. Make sure you reach your intended destination by adjusting your course as you go. *Ditch* those things that are taking you further away from your target and *Do* more of what is working for you, to make sure you stay on track.

DISCover how to work smart, make decisions as a team and how to monitor and measure for successful results.

I often imagine all the elements of my business as lighting up on an enormous business dashboard. Everything is there: from your cash flow and your budget to your sales and marketing. When things are going well all the lights are green; but the troublesome areas tend to flash amber or red in my mind, alerting me to where I need to pay attention. Hopefully I have anticipated the danger moments and will already have a strategy in place for dealing with them – but if they catch me unawares, a more drastic approach will be needed.

> Some years ago my husband and I were running a chain of health clubs. We sold one for several hundred thousand pounds to an individual who believed in the absolute power of customer service. He believed it to the extent that he felt it was not necessary to sell because, as he said, 'If the product is good enough, people will buy'. With this in mind, he decided to drop the sales process and allow the sales team just to give people a tour of the club and a price list. Unfortunately, because he made a fundamental change to one of the key elements in the success of the club, it soon went into a downward spiral. He would not acknowledge that the removal of the sales procedure was the reason for the club's decline and within twelve months needed to sell the club before it closed. My husband and I bought the club back for £65,000, inherited the same team, reinstalled the systems and procedures that had previously worked and the sales and profits responded accordingly, to the extent that we were able to sell it yet again some twelve months later. You have to keep your eye on all aspects of the business at all times. The decision-making lesson here is 'If it ain't broke, don't fix it'. Profit and sales go hand in hand, along with excellent customer service, of course. You won't achieve one without the other. It is an essential rule of business management.

KEEP CALM AND CARRY ON

When the unexpected happens in the workplace, members of my team often say to me 'How can you stay so calm? What if everything goes wrong?' My answer is almost always: 'Everything will be fine; and even if it isn't, we will deal with it – so the outcome will still be fine.' Facing challenges keeps us strong.

Mental resilience or toughness is what separates the great from the 'could be' great. As a leader you need to remain calm and clear under pressure. Worry is just a way of programming your brain to be negative. As Eleanor Roosevelt once said: 'People are like tea bags. You don't know how strong they are going to be until you drop them in hot water.'

The Do It! or Ditch It approach to management focuses a great deal on clarity of purpose and open communication. The clue to success lies in being extremely clear about personal goals and expectations – including your own – and to have in place clear processes for monitoring and measuring results on an ongoing basis. When the going gets tough, I find it useful to rise above a situation and imagine looking down at what is really going on. From that 'big picture' viewpoint I ask myself: 'If X happened; what would I do next? Or if Y happened; what would I do?' Viewing the situation from above can help you to detach yourself from associated feelings, allowing a clear perspective.

DEVELOP A 'DO IT!' WAY OF WORKING (WOW)

Every decision you make has an impact not only on short-term motivation but also on the long-term direction and outcome of your plans and goals. It is not just the decisions themselves that are important, but maintaining momentum and consistency of delivery, too. Very often, the reason a business isn't working effectively is because the business owner isn't. That doesn't mean to say that they aren't working hard. It is more likely that they aren't working on the right things within the business. Talent alone won't make you a success. Neither will being in the right place at the right time, unless you are prepared and ready to take positive action.

Those who are successful in business tend to be single-minded and focused on the end result. They will focus on the detail when they need to, but in general are able to delegate tasks that steal their time and concentrate instead on those commercially relevant decisions that will drive the business forward more quickly. But how does that apply on a day-to-day basis? If you are working on your own, what is the best way to accomplish your aims? How can you stop yourself from wasting time on things that don't matter in the short term, while keeping everyone happy?

 **DO IT!**

TEN GREAT WOWs

- Set goals for everything you do.
- Plan your actions daily – and stick to your own schedule.
- Prioritise tasks that add value to your business.
- Delegate tasks that could be done by someone else (possibly for less money).
- Communicate clearly with others and make your expectations clear.
- Be self-disciplined and maintain a 'can-do' attitude.
- Look after your health: exercise daily and get enough sleep.
- Don't put off making tough decisions.
- Make every decision count towards your long-term goal.
- Say 'No' to anything that will distract from your immediate priority.

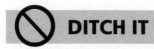

DITCH IT

TEN WORRYING WOWs

- Doing everything yourself.
- Relying on one customer for the majority of your business.
- Relying on one supplier, or a single route to market.
- Spending more time on administration than generating new business.
- Tending to start new projects before you have completed others.
- Never getting the results you want from your team or your suppliers.
- Not making a profit/working long hours for low return.
- Customers/clients owe you money.
- Poor health/short of sleep/low energy.
- Lack of enjoyment in your work.

> *'Focus on doing those things that add value to your business and delegate non-essential tasks to other people.'*

Stress and pressure tend to develop when we feel out of control of a situation. When the red lights flash on the business management dashboard it is usually because the business owner has been working hard but in the wrong areas; maybe through lack of time, or inexperience, or because they have put their trust in someone else to deliver results and something has gone wrong. Red lights can take you immediately from the comfort zone into the panic zone. To move things forward in a way that puts you back in control requires a cool head and a focused mind.

1. Look back from the future: re-enter that time machine and revisit your end goal. What priority decision do you need to take today to ensure that your goal remains attainable?

2. Focus your mind and test that decision on a scale of 1 to 10. How much closer will that decision take you? How much further away will it take you?

3. If useful, apply the SWOT test. What are the strengths or weaknesses of your proposed action?

4. What would other people do? Consider the pros and cons from a DISC walk perspective.

5. Make your mind up: Do it! or Ditch it. Take action, cut loose from the panic zone and move forward into stretch. There is nothing to be gained from dwelling on mistakes and everything to be lost if you lose your confidence at a crucial moment.

DISCover YOUR APPROACH TO MANAGEMENT DECISION-MAKING

Each of the DISC styles has its own strengths and weaknesses when it comes to making management decisions and it is the way we react under pressure that will ultimately impact on the future success of your idea or your business. It can be useful to recognise your own management style under pressure so that you can consciously modify your approach – especially in team meetings and briefing sessions.

D

High D-styles make fast decisions.

Management style:
- Directs.
- Will want to act fast.
- Will act alone if necessary.
- Does not need consensus before making a decision.
- Will want results fast.
- Will worry about the detail later.
- Has confidence in their own ability.
- Likes change.
- The bigger the challenge, the greater the motivation.

Needs to:
- Listen more carefully.
- Take on board others' concerns.
- Be realistic about time frames.

DANGEROUS DECISIONS?
- Under pressure, fear of failure or exploitation may lead to:
- Over-trading; expanding too fast.
- Taking action with inadequate information.
- Being overly competitive regardless of risk.
- Belief in own infallibility.

I

High I-styles see endless possibilities.

Management style:
- Collaborative and persuasive.
- Positive and optimistic.
- Shares responsibility.
- Announces good news fast.
- Focuses on sales and promotion.
- Looks to others to manage and complete tasks.
- Is ready to learn from others.
- Has an original and imaginative approach to decision-making.
- Likes to be original.
- Seeks joint ventures.

Needs to:
- Follow up words with practical actions.
- Focus on one project at a time.
- Keep to schedules.

DANGEROUS DECISIONS?
- Under pressure, fear of rejection or loss of popularity may lead to:
- Over-committing. An inability to say 'No'.
- Making decisions based on personalities without checking the facts.
- Belief in own power of persuasion.
- Being over-optimistic.

C	S
C-styles take a long time to act.	**S-styles maintain the status quo.**
Management style:	**Management style:**
• Wants facts and figures to support every decision.	• Needs to know that all processes have been thought through before making a decision.
• Will want all to adhere to rules and regulations.	• Needs to know that everyone is happy with the decision.
• May communicate decisions via memo and data rather than in person.	• Needs to know that there will be minimal disruption to the business.
• Unlikely to take action unless legally watertight.	• Needs to know that others have done something similar and succeeded.
	• Needs to know there will be little chance of failure.
Needs to:	**Needs to:**
• Focus on working in a more relational manner.	• Learn to feel comfortable in the stretch zone.
• Communicate directly and lead from the front.	• Plan the short term with the long-term goal in mind.
• Trust that there is more than one 'right' decision.	• Trust that the team will adjust to change.
DANGEROUS DECISIONS?	**DANGEROUS DECISIONS?**
• Under pressure, fear of getting it wrong may lead to:	• Under pressure, fear of loss of security may lead to:
• Decisions being made by process of elimination rather than choosing preferred outcome.	• Being too fearful of change to take a risk.
• Working in isolation to try to solve problems rather than as part of a team.	• Collaborating to the extent that the goal becomes unclear.
• Belief that an outcome that is less than perfect = failure.	• Belief that the outcome is possible without changing anything.

DO IT! OR DITCH IT DECISION-MAKING IN MEETINGS

Good ideas can come from anywhere, but it is the role of the business owner to decide which ones to focus on and drive them through. The Do It! or Ditch It tools have an important role to play in making effective decisions:

As the business owner, it is useful to do a DISC run (or a brisk walk) to say to yourself:

D: Let's do it!

I: Who can I work with?

S: What are the risks?

C: Let's run the numbers …

I think of new business development as going on a business journey. Each team member and every function has a part to play. In my own company I am usually the one who comes up with the strategic ideas. I'll then run the numbers past our finance controller before deciding whether or not we are going ahead.

It's important to announce new ideas to the team in a very positive way, to ensure buy-in and get everyone on board. We will then look together at how we can make the idea even better and break it down into separate steps. This is often known as 'chunking'.

One of the reasons that many people are daunted by decisions relating to new ventures is that they find the process of breaking down the big picture into smaller, manageable tasks quite difficult. As a result they procrastinate or may never get started at all. Others may get so bogged down in detail that they lose sight of the overall objective.

This is where working with the team becomes useful. Each person looks at the information necessary, or the actions we need to take within their own area of responsibility, and we then come back together to compare notes and decide on the next steps. In effect, we take the 'customer journey' and consider how the new business idea will be experienced from the customer's point of view. Every area of the customer experience is considered, from the website experience, to the buying experience, to administration and so on – covering all the bases.

This is an essential stage for me because I tend to be very big-picture and I know I may miss some of the detail. So together, as a team, we plan the whole customer experience and how each team member contributes to that journey. Ask your team to help put together a business SWOT, so the Strengths and Weaknesses are properly identified, and the Opportunities and threats can be built in as part of your business plan.

Opportunities are like aeroplanes on the radar: you want to keep them in sight and you may want to line up three or four for landing, but you don't call them in to land until you are ready. In terms of deciding which actions to take, the considerations are:

- Which are easiest to do?
- Which will make a financial difference?
- Which are the most cost-effective?
- Which would need further resources?

Over a period of time, all the Opportunities can be included as part of your business – but don't try to do too many things at once (or lose sight of the Opportunities by filing them away).

MONITOR AND MEASURE PERFORMANCE

Most business decisions relate to performance, profit, or both. To get an accurate idea of how well a strategy is working it is important to monitor and measure every aspect of what you are trying to achieve. This means measuring and monitoring yourself and *your* motivation as well as the performance of the business and those around you.

Many companies use Key Performance Indicators (KPIs) as a benchmark for evaluating different elements of individual and departmental performance. These will vary according to the needs and aims of each business. Setting KPIs for each role and each task provides an extremely useful standard by which you and your team can monitor and measure progress more quickly – which in turn drives the decisions that you make each day. Without having a standard in place each decision takes more time.

The sales funnel is an example of an effective dashboard measurement tool frequently used in many sales and marketing environments:

The marketing campaign is launched.

There is a response to the campaign, prospects are generated and data is captured.

Prospects express an interest in the product or service and the sales team takes them through a process.

Sales are made.

You now have a client base.

You work hard to keep your clients (excellent product and customer service etc).

Once the marketing campaign is launched you can then monitor the 'numbers'.

- How many leads/prospects does the campaign produce?
- How many leads/prospects are you/your team able to 'pitch'?

- How many sales are made?
- How many customers do you retain/get repeat business from?

If you have employees, it is useful to ensure that each person has individual objectives and that they understand the KPIs for their area of the business. Do they know what and how to monitor and measure their daily activities in order to be successful?

For example:

In the health club environment I found this tool extremely useful to assess individual sales team effectiveness:

Sales team member 1

- Has a bank of one hundred leads to make contact with.
- Speaks to forty people.
- Makes ten appointments from the calls.
- Six of the appointed people show up.
- Four of the people join the club.

This means that sales team member 1 has the following KPIs:

- Call to appointment ratio = 25 per cent.
- Appointment to 'show' ratio = 60 per cent.
- Presentation to sale ratio = 66 per cent.

This information can help a manager/owner understand where the strengths and possible challenge areas are which, in turn, can help identify possible training needs.

For example:

For sales team member 1 to do more business he or she needs to do some or all of the following:

- Make more calls.
- Improve telephone technique to make more appointments.

- Improve appointment confirmation technique to improve show-up rate
- Improve sales presentation technique to get more people to join.

By monitoring these types of numbers, benchmarks can be set for the sales team, which may well change as the team improves their techniques through training.

For example:

- Call to appointment ratio = 30 per cent.
- Appointment to show ratio = 60 per cent.
- Presentation to sale ratio = 70 per cent.

HOW TO ENCOURAGE A BUSINESS-OWNER MENTALITY

It is so much easier to make your business a success if those you employ and work with have as much belief in you and your business as you do. In an ideal world every one of your team members or employees would care as much about the outcomes of their task and your business as you do. If everybody within and connected to your business shared your business-owner mentality, poor customer service or inefficient work would become a thing of the past.

To develop this approach your team needs to feel trusted. As we all know, trust is earned over time. The skill lies in allowing your team members the opportunity and the environment to earn such trust. Brief them well – and then let them get on with the task. Review and appraise at the end of the task, so that they can learn more about what you want and expect from the feedback.

If you communicate openly and lead by example, you can encourage an ownership mentality in every person who works for the organisation. This is really important. If everyone feels a part of your brand or business they will care about it being a success as much as you do, which will help to safeguard your profits and make others feel that they share in your success.

If your team were paying the bills, would they leave so many lights on? Would they overstock slow-selling goods? Would they delay returning a sales call instantly? Would they be rude to customers? It's unlikely.

Shared values and goals are important in a business, especially in a small or start-up business. If you find you are working at cross purposes with a key member of your team the consequences can be time-consuming and exhausting. By encouraging others to understand your business strategy and take partial responsibility for the costs of running the business you are more likely to create a team that thinks for itself and makes decisions that support your goals.

As a business owner, knowing that your team are giving their best and commited to the best interests of you and your business, is very reassuring. I had transparent evidence of this when I first embarked on launching EBA with James Caan. It is hard for me to imagine how I would have set up EBA without my business manager, Amelia Scott, on board. Her dedication to the project was incredible and she matched every hour of the day that I worked, which often meant being focused on the project until eleven o'clock at night and at weekends to make sure we delivered our plan. She couldn't have worked harder, been more dedicated to the task, or more proud when we launched our first event. She gave, unquestioningly, 'whatever it takes': that is the sign of an ownership mentality. It is a characteristic that the whole team show, especially when under pressure.

 **DO IT!**

TRIED AND TESTED DECISIONS THAT ENCOURAGE OWNERSHIP MENTALITY

- **Decide to trust your team.** If you want to encourage others to develop an ownership mentality you need to decide to trust them and to involve them in what you are aiming to achieve. Trust is earned over a period of time and by results but, if you hire people with the right skills, train them and brief them well, then you can afford to let them get on with the job.

- **Encourage others to make decisions.** If a member of your team is constantly asking your opinion rather than showing initiative, he or she may lack confidence or sense that you like things done in a particular way. Try asking, 'What do you think?', 'What would you do?' or letting them learn from their own efforts before offering your opinion. It may take longer to get the task done initially, but eventually people will start to come up with their own solutions. When you start to trust people, they start to believe in themselves and will grow into the role – and feel more loyal to you and your business.

- **Be transparent.** You can't expect people to meet a target that they cannot see. I believe it is important to be very clear with your team about the financial goals you have for the business and the financial state of the business. That way, your team is more likely to understand your reasons for **not** doing something. When deciding not to buy something for the business, explain why, and what the financial impact would have been. Developing a business-owner mentality requires people to take financial responsibility for their decisions – and to consider the bigger picture.

- **Show your enthusiasm.** Positivity breeds positivity, and it helps team morale if the leader is able to remain consistently upbeat. If you speak respectfully to, and about, your customers or clients, other people will do so, too. If, on the other hand, you tend to mutter a few choice words after putting down the phone because someone has annoyed you, your team will be more likely to be disrespectful, too. Start to share different elements of your business plan and get the team involved and excited about your business. Good ideas thrive in a supportive and creative environment. The more you show enthusiasm, the more acceptable it will be for others to be passionate about their own roles.

- **Show your team that you care about them.** No relationship will survive if it is one-sided. Your team needs to know that you care about their welfare, just as you want them to care about the welfare of the business. If you make sure that people feel they are special, as well as part of something special, they will begin to care about it as much as you do.

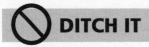 **DITCH IT**

- **Avoid hovering and micro-managing.** Once you have briefed someone and are confident that they have understood what is required, allow them the flexibility to interpret your requirements and add their own flair – provided the end result meets the criteria required.
- **Do not criticise in front of others.** If you want to speak to a member of your team about a sensitive matter, keep it private – and ensure that you give them a chance to have their say.
- **Don't tolerate poor performance.** It is vital to take action early with regard to poor performance. All too often people put off taking team members to task; if a problem goes unaddressed, it frequently becomes bigger and harder to deal with. When dealing with poor performance, you will need to understand how the issue has arisen – is it down to lack of

understanding as to the task (communication problem); lack
of time (prioritising), lack of ability (training issue) or lack of
urgency (failure to see the importance of the task)? Only when
you understand how the issue has arisen can you know how to
address it.

COMMUNICATION MATTERS

One of the best management decisions you can make is to
schedule time to talk to those on the front line of your business,
because they can give you candid feedback about how the
business is being received by customers. It doesn't pay to cut
yourself off from complaints and bad news.

Ask your customers whether your outlet is delivering to their
expectations. If you lead a team, ask them how you are doing and
whether they have concerns or any suggestions for improvement.
Let them speak and believe the honesty of what they have to say
– no matter how inconvenient. Behind every comment there is
an opportunity to do things better.

In my coaching business I continue to deliver training sessions
personally because I don't want to lose touch with the people
who make up our business. For my own benefit and in the future
interests of the company, I need to find out whether we are still
offering what people want and where new opportunities lie.

I am passionate about business, but I know all too well that
unless leaders have a good rapport with their people and work
effectively as a team, launching any kind of strategy is going to
be an uphill struggle. You need to look after those on the front
line and listen to their views if you want to succeed.

ACCOUNT FOR YOUR TIME AND YOUR PROFIT WILL FOLLOW

Everyone has the same twenty-four hours in a day, so why is it that successful business owners and leaders are able to achieve so much where many others are left struggling to complete a few tasks? Ultimately, the story of your life will depend on how you use the time you have been given. Your success in business depends on how you manage your own and other people's time. It is our most precious business resource and the one that is the most easily squandered.

Time management is, of course, self-management. It is a combination of planning, realism and self-awareness. But to control time we first need to understand our relationship with it. It may seem harmless to say time and time again (excuse the pun) 'I don't have time', 'I can't make time', 'Time just runs away', or 'Time is not on my side', but these expressions betray a belief that time is in control of you, rather than the other way around. Instead, try saying 'I can always make time'. Think about time as if you can manufacture it at will and you will always have enough.

Those who get more done tend to stay in control and focused on their use of time, even if something unexpected pops up that they would rather be doing.

> *'Do what you are doing; and ditch the short-term distractions. That way there will be time enough to achieve everything you need to do.'*

Many working professionals find that at least part of their working day is compromised by unwanted distractions or having to listen to other people's needs. It can be hard to redirect a conversation if it is a customer or client who has a need to talk:

but you need to remember that your time is valuable, and you need to treat it like the commodity it is.

Penny Power of Ecademy identifies that managing her mind rather than her time is the key to getting the best results from each day. Peter Thomson takes a more goal-centred approach.

 **DO IT!**

PENNY POWER KNOWS IT IS ALL IN THE MIND

'Managing my mind is what takes most time, not managing my time! If I manage my mind I am able to build my business with the right noise, people and intention. When I become task-driven I become hard to meet, hard to communicate with and I lose my identity. Time management implies setting up filters and being controlling. This stops people getting through to you. The best way to manage your time is to manage your mind. Ask, "What do I want to achieve?" not "What time shall I allocate to every task!"'

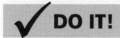 **DO IT!**

PETER THOMSON TAKES A GOAL-CENTRED APPROACH

'Always use a do list; always have goals. Without goals you'll never distinguish between urgent and important tasks and you'll end up doing all the urgent ones and leaving the important ones. If you don't have your own goals – your actions will always be about fulfilling someone else's.'

DITCH IT

DITCH THE TIME STEALERS

- **Social media.** Twitter, Facebook and other social networking sites are worth every minute of the time you spend on them if you are developing a marketing campaign – and are invaluable for building relationships with customers. Stay time-wise and use them productively so they don't eat into your working day.

DIFFICULT DECISIONS

The people-related decisions that you make in business may have to be acted upon fairly quickly and they can be uncomfortable ones to make, from the personal – letting go a casual worker who helped build up your business in the early stages – to the formal – taking someone through a process to formally dismiss them.

Most people dislike conflict in the workplace. Why can't we all just rub along harmoniously and get the job done? Unfortunately, sometimes people either consistently underperform or they behave inappropriately. There are many laws and procedures in place to protect the rights of the individual and to ensure that employers act appropriately when asking them to leave. They were hard won and it is good that they are in place, but sometimes business owners can become so put off by the process that they will put up with poor behaviour, rather than seizing the nettle and letting someone go.

If a person is not doing their job, you will eventually lose some of your good people as well as the one you would like to leave. When the pressure is on, you are only as strong as your weakest link. So often when I am coaching someone and a weak member of staff leaves a company, I will ask: 'How long have they been underperforming?' The answer is often 'Months, years ...' A conscious decision was never made to get rid of them, but when they do eventually leave, everyone says, 'Thank goodness for that, didn't like working with them anyway.' So why didn't you do something about it?

The reasons for hanging on to someone can be complex. It may be a case of 'Better the devil you know', or the hassle of getting in somebody new; the owner may realise there is a bigger problem and think, 'Whoever I get, the same thing will happen'.

It may help to think of your team as 'going for gold'. If you were in charge of an Olympic squad you wouldn't be able to carry passengers. Everyone would have to earn their place on the team, based on merit. It should be no different in business. It is a pleasure to work with people you enjoy being around, but at the end of the day you are in business to make money and it is all about the quality of the end result. Even the largest organisation will find it financially challenging and counter-productive to carry a member of the team who is not pulling their weight.

DISCIPLINING AND DISMISSAL

The D-style approach to discipline and dismissal

D-styles will generally be unemotional and direct when dealing with matters of discipline. They will 'tell it as it is' without dressing it up and will let you know the consequences of a repeat offence. Often they will offer training and support but will expect you to say whether you want it or not. If you don't take the offer and mess up again, then expect the worst!

D-styles can be extremely direct to the point of being blunt in some cases. They can be unaware of or unconcerned about the effect this may have on the more 'sensitive' styles.

D-styles may not always want to follow time-consuming disciplinary procedures, which can be an expensive mistake if the team member wishes to go to an industrial tribunal.

The I-style discipline and dismissal

I-styles want to be popular – disciplining people will (in their eyes) affect their popularity and so they may well delay taking action. I-styles can sometimes be so nice about the disciplinary procedure that team members are unaware that they have had one!

I-styles are relational and will often attempt to avoid formal procedures in favour of a relaxed, informal approach. This can lead to difficulty later on if the situation becomes legal, as set procedures will not have been followed.

The S-style discipline and dismissal

S-styles are generally relational by nature and will not enjoy taking team members through the disciplinary process. While they may well delay taking action, ultimately they will complete the task in a sympathetic manner.

S-styles will often look for alternatives to taking action and not do so until they are certain they have all the facts. They will not want to get caught out or feel awkward in what they perceive will be a sensitive time.

The C-style discipline and dismissal

C-styles will conduct matters in a formal manner and everything will be 'done by the book'. C-styles generally like to manage by set rules and regulations and may sometimes come across as a little 'cool' inter-personally. When dealing with matters of discipline and dismissal, they will act in a logical manner and see things through professionally.

If you do decide to dismiss a member of staff or a supplier, you need to have the strength to stick to your decision, because in the cold light of day, when you are looking someone in the eye, it can be all too easy to feel like backtracking. There is no easy way to let someone go. It is human nature to like people and to become attached to them, which is why making a decision based on personality alone is too difficult and usually inappropriate. Making a decision based on your commercial priorities usually makes the outcome very clear.

 **DO IT!**

THE TEN RULES FOR DIFFICULT DECISION-MAKING

1. Gather all of the facts.
2. Take advice from an HR expert.
3. Rehearse exactly what you are going to say in advance.
4. Allow the person to have their say.
5. Evaluate.
6. Make a decision.
7. Tell someone else about the decision you have made.
8. Schedule your action.
9. Stick to your decision.
10. DO IT!

Keep emotion out of it. If you have to give negative feedback, don't make it personal. Stick to the behaviour and the consequence for your business.

JAMIE CONSTABLE – CUT HARD, BUT ONLY CUT ONCE

In his role as a turnaround expert, Jamie has a lot of experience of staffing matters. 'If you need to cut back staff, you need to cut hard – so that you won't need to cut again. But only ever cut once. You can't keep doing it. Make the business leaner than it's ever been – to the point where you feel you've overdone it. You can then say to your staff, I've had to do this, but now your jobs are safe and we can concentrate on running this business profitably. But get the workforce to a level where they are as lean as they can possibly be.

Identify the "stars" of your business. Who are the people in your business who can really make a success of it? There are usually some really good people in the organisation who have the knowledge and the ability to help your business grow, if given the opportunity. These people are your champions. Incentivise them and work with them. They are the ones who will make the business come through the tough times.'

SELF-MANAGEMENT – YOUR KEY TO BETTER DECISION-MAKING

Leadership requires self-discipline and self-management at all times. Other people are looking to you to set the pace and to make the wise decisions that make things happen. You embody the qualities that your company represents. To that extent you will need to be clear and consistent in your approach – and as tough on yourself as you are likely to be on others. Self-management is the key to effective business management.

The life cycle for new products, ideas and even business relationships is shorter these days because the speed of innovation and change is happening so fast. To survive in business, decisions need to be sharp and focused. You need to be more ready than ever before to seize opportunities when they arise. My advice is, don't just wait for opportunities to present themselves, decide what you want and go for it. Recognise what you need to do to get yourself ready to take action – and take steps to develop the business skills that you currently lack. Projects, tasks and opportunities may lie ahead of you that will demand business skills that you currently lack. Face up to those areas where your skills may be lacking, and factor personal training into your budget. Losing out on an opportunity simply because you don't feel ready for the challenge will send you straight back into the comfort zone and it will take longer to take the step forward to change next time around. (See the Appendix on page 264 for insights into how a business mentor can fast-track your personal development.)

DO IT! OR DITCH IT CHECKLIST

WHEN?

Managing your business

Try using the simple scale that follows to assess your attitude to managing your business. Consider each characteristic below and rate by marking where on the line your state of mind lies. Do you feel closer to the right-hand column, or the left-hand column?

This exercise does not evaluate how good you are at business management. There are no 'good feelings' or 'bad feelings' and no rights or wrongs. It is a way to assess your frame of mind.

On balance, are you in a 'Do It!' frame of mind? Or is that critical voice inside your head suggesting you should 'Ditch it' because it feels more as if your business is managing you than the other way around?

CHECK YOUR MINDSET

On a scale of 1 to 10, how close are you to your goal?

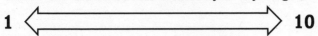

1   10

The 'Ditch It' Warning Signs	The 'Do It!' Mindset
I prefer to go with the flow	I am very goal-oriented
I take stock from time to time	I begin the day with an action plan
My team know what they are doing	I check in with my team daily
I leave people to get on with their jobs	I delegate, but follow through
Meetings are a waste of time	Meetings are useful provided there is an agenda and actions agreed
I am tired all the time	I feel constantly energised by my work
The joy has gone out of my work	I really love what I do
I can never say 'no'	I try to say 'yes' on my terms
I expect my team to be self-disciplined	I like to lead by example
The old ways are the best	I am constantly working to improve the way I do things

WHAT ACTIONS WILL TAKE YOU ONE STEP CLOSER TO YOUR GOAL?

WRITE THEM HERE

STEP 8: DO IT! OR DITCH IT

Making a decision

TAKING STOCK

'Business is a behaviour. We can control how we think, how we act and what we do to improve our chances of success.'

Step 8: DO IT! OR DITCH IT decisions are not just related to business; they will become your philosophy for life. Every decision you make leads ultimately to success as you reach your goal or disappointment and review as you reach a place where your goal is no longer achievable. Step 8 is about taking stock, deciding whether to make ongoing plans, to adjust your strategy or to draw a line; it is about maintaining growth, planning to expand or changing track. The decision and the choice are yours.

Every idea and every business needs constant re-evaluation. The final Do It! or Ditch It step is about making difficult decisions: whether to adjust your expectations, reassess your idea or abandon your plan altogether.

Using the DISC walk can help you to face your fears and see off the pressure. It will help you to understand what makes you move towards or away from your goal; to decide consciously to keep moving forward or not.

DO IT! OR DITCH IT MOMENTS

Every process in business has its own flow and momentum. If that momentum is not maintained at a steady pace, the idea will lose its energy and fade away. Someone has to drive that pace

– and that person needs to be you. If you have a project on the blocks that keeps stalling, take a good hard look at why it is not happening.

- Is the commercial model wrong?
- Is the timing off?
- Are the key players involved the right people to make it happen?

Self-sabotage, procrastination and over-commitment are all warning signs – and the true cost of not making decisions stick.

To help you decide whether to Do It! or Ditch It, revisit your decision-making tools:

Enter the stretch zone

Ask yourself:

'What is my greatest fear?'

'What is preventing me from taking action at the moment?'

'What do I need to do to change my perspective and stretch my comfort zone?'

'Am I willing to enter the stretch zone to get to where I want to go?'

Look back from the future

Ask yourself:

'Where do I want to be tomorrow, next week, next year? '

'What do I need to do today to ensure that I am on plan and heading in the right direction?'

'What am I willing to give up (what fear, what habit, what behaviour) in order to fulfil my goal?'

Review the SWOT spot

Ask yourself:

'What are my Strengths and Weaknesses?'

'How can I turn them into Opportunities?'

'What action can I take to diminish the Threats?'

Focus your mind

On a scale of 1 to 10, ask yourself:

'Will this action take me closer to or further away from my goal?'
'How likely am I to take this action today?'
'Do I want to take this action today?'
'What do I need in order to take this action?'
'Will I ever take this action?'

To be successful you must be able to have a PASSION for action; to have a BELIEF in the IDEA; to recognise the right OPPORTUNITY; to take appropriate ACTION; to ensure FOLLOW-THROUGH and drive the project to COMPLETION. If any of these pieces are missing, the picture is not complete and success may always be just out of reach.

If you haven't made time to plan it, and you haven't the time or resources to do it – then perhaps now is the time to dig deep and ditch it – so you can begin to focus on those things that you *can and will make happen.*

Now ask yourself

What are your actions going to be in the next:

Month?

Week?

Day?

Hour?

Minute?

What are you waiting for?

1...   2...   3...

 DO IT!

OR

 **DITCH IT**

APPENDIX

A BUSINESS MENTOR CAN JUMP-START YOUR SUCCESS

(How to find one, choose one, use one)

You don't need a licence to start a business. There is no law that says you need to know how to sell or understand a balance sheet though common sense suggests some form of experience would be useful. The myth is that 'anyone can do it'. And the truth is that anyone can – but many businesses founder in the attempt.

If you were planning an expedition to the Arctic, where hidden dangers could jeopardise progress and where the climate could change at a moment's notice, would you go without an experienced guide? Probably not. The same applies when starting in business. A business mentor can guide you and help you to navigate your path to success.

Five ways that a business mentor can help you and your business to succeed are as follows. A mentor:

1. Can help guide you through potential minefields.
2. Can provide perspective and will see things objectively.
3. Will have years of experience and will have learned from their own mistakes.
4. Can help you get where you are going to, but faster.
5. May also choose to introduce you to his or her contacts and resources.

HOW TO FIND ONE

Ask any start-up entrepreneur who they would most like to have as a mentor and most will list assorted dragons from the BBC's *Den*, Lord Sugar or Sir Richard Branson. But there are many other dragons out there, many of them running successful businesses in your home town or local area.

To find a mentor, start networking within your business community. Ask yourself what specifically you want (and need) to learn. How could the arrangement be reciprocated? Some of the most valuable mentors will probably be in areas that complement your own.

HOW TO CHOOSE ONE

There is no formula for choosing a mentor: the ideal mentor is simply the one who is right for you and your business, depending on your needs at the time. An effective mentor will help you to regain focus, fire you up with enthusiasm and help you to see with greater clarity.

Successful businesspeople can often provide more incisive insights in ten minutes than can be gleaned from personal experience in three years. I have had some wonderful mentors in my life and also enjoy, and benefit from, mentoring others. I am a great believer in the rule of reciprocation. Don't consider taking on a mentor for yourself unless you, too, are willing to be a mentor. Everyone in business can benefit from having a mentor. Many entrepreneurs have more than one mentor. Even mentors have mentors!

HOW TO USE ONE

Ask yourself what you need a mentor for. What resources are missing from your business? You may want more than one and your mentors may change as your needs change, as you absorb knowledge and gain in experience.

There are broadly three kinds of mentors: short-term troubleshooters, specialist advisers and long-term experts.

Short-term mentors

There are times in the development of every business when an injection of short-term expertise is required. You may be thinking of selling the company and need help with valuation; perhaps you want to launch a new product line, buy or move to new premises, take part in a merger, or have some tough restructuring decisions to take. Short-term mentors provide a steady hand to guide you through unfamiliar territory to a successful outcome. They are unlikely to be involved in your business long-term.

Specialist mentors

Specialist mentors are usually involved on an ongoing basis. It is not unusual for a business to involve two or three mentors at the same time, each providing different skills and experience. They may include your bank manager, your accountant, a business adviser; or they may be individuals who bring valuable commercial experience to your business.

Long-term mentors

Some mentors share their wisdom over a long period. The ideal mentor for this role will have at least five to ten years more experience than the business owner and may well have knowledge or experience in the same field. This type of mentor is like a non-executive director. His involvement may last a few years, or for the lifetime of the business.

What mentors are not:

A mentor is not a business consultant.

A mentor is not a coach.

A mentor is not a counsellor.

A mentor does not run your business.

You run your business. Mentors are there only to offer the advice and insights that you ask for.

The advantage of embarking on your journey with a mentor from the outset is that he or she will help you to anticipate obstacles in advance, and show you how to navigate well-charted waters – to speed up your route to success.

For further information contact:

The Entrepreneurs' Business Academy

www.the-eba.com

FURTHER RESOURCES

Association of Chartered Certified Accountants (ACCA)
www.accaglobal.com

British Chambers of Commerce (BCC)
www.britishchambers.org.uk
www.thebusiness-startup.co.uk

Business Start-Up Show
www.bstartup.com

Companies House
www.companieshouse.gov.uk
Contact centre: +44 (0)303 1234 500

Chartered Institute of Management Accountants (CIMA)
www.cimaglobal.com

Department of Business Industry and Skills (BIS)
www.bis.gov.uk

Directgov
www.direct.gov.uk

Entrepreneurs' Business Academy
www.the-eba.com

Federation of Small Businesses
www.fsb.org.uk

Health and Safety Executive

www.hse.gov.uk

Ask an expert: 0845 3 450 055

HM Revenue and Customs

www.hmrc.gov.uk

Newly self-employed helpline: 0845 915 4515

New employer helpline: 0845 607 0143

Institute of Chartered Accountants in England and Wales (ICAEW)

www.icaewfirms.co.uk

Institute of Chartered Accountants in Ireland (ICAI)

www.icai.ie

Institute of Chartered Accountants of Scotland (ICAS)

www.icas.org.uk

Investors in People

www.investorsinpeople.co.uk

Intellectual Property Office

www.ipo.gov.uk

Enquiries: 0845 9 500 505.

Law Society of England and Wales

www.lawsociety.org.uk

Law Society of Scotland

www.lawscot.org.uk

Peter Jones' National Enterprise Academy

www.thenea.org

PRIME (The Prince's Initiative for Mature Enterprise)

www.primeinitiative.co.uk

Prime Business Club

www.primebusinessclub.com

Prince's Trust

www.princes-trust.org.uk

Survey Monkey

www.surveymonkey.com

A service that designs customer feedback questionnaires. Many of their resources are free.

For further information about Do It! or Ditch It techniques and free downloads, visit www.BevJames.com

FINANCIAL GLOSSARY

Accruals   Accounting reflection of cost incurred but not yet invoiced, or not subject to invoice. Payroll is a common example.

Asset   Property which will bring some future economic benefit.

Balance sheet   This is the presentation of what your business owns, what it owes and what its shareholders have put in.

Breakeven   Where revenue matches cost and profit is nil.

Capital   The investment made in a business.

Capitalise   To treat a purchase as an asset rather than an expense, usually because you will use it for an extended period.

Cost centre   Non-revenue segment or division of the business for which costs are segregated.

Cost of sales   This is the cost to the business of the goods or services which you have sold in a period.

Creditor days   The number of days' worth of purchases equal to the amount you owe your trade creditors.

Current asset   An asset which is expected to be turned into cash within twelve months.

Current liability   A liability which is expected to be repaid, or for which payment can be demanded within twelve months.

Dashboard   An up-to-date summary of business measurements.

Debtor days   The number of days of sales equal to the amount your customers owe you.

Depreciation   The accounting expense which spreads the cost of fixed assets over their useful lives.

Double entry   Technique for recording events and transactions in books of account.

EBITDA   Earnings Before Interest, Tax, Depreciation and Amortisation. Often used as a proxy for operating cash flow.

EBITDAR   EBITDA before rent costs. This is used to compare businesses with lots of property – such as retailers – because some businesses own their properties while others rent them.

Equity   The owner's investment in a business together with accumulated profits and losses.

Financial accounts   Set of financial statements which follow legal or regulated formats and contents.

Fixed assets   Assets which are intended for long-term use in the business.

Gearing   Proportion of funding which comes from borrowing rather than equity.

Goodwill   The value of a business less the value of its assets and liabilities.

HMRC   Her Majesty's Revenue and Customs. UK tax authority, formed from a merger of Inland Revenue and Customs & Excise.

Income statement   Summary presentation, on an accruals basis, of all the revenue and expenses for a set period. Also called the profit and loss account.

IP   Intellectual Property.

IPR   Intellectual Property Rights. Includes things like patents and copyright.

KPI   Key Performance Indicator.

Ltd   Limited company. Companies are legally separate from their shareholders, giving shareholders limited liability.

Management accounts   Internal financial statements.

Materiality   Concept that only numbers over a certain size are important.

Over-trading   The cause of business failure where business runs out of cash as it grows, even though it may be profitable.

Personal financial guarantee   A personal agreement to take on third-party liability. For example, to take on the debt of another person if they default on a loan.

Plc   Public limited company. Has minimum capital requirements.

Prepayment   Accounting reflection of payment having been made in advance of the expense being incurred. The opposite of an accrual. Rent and insurance are common examples.

Profit and Loss (P&L) account   See Income statement.

Provision   An accounting reduction in the value of an asset which is expected not to be fully recoverable.

Small Companies Rate   The Corporation Tax rate (21 per cent) applied to a business which has taxable profits of less than £1,500,000 (valid to 31 March 2011).

Sole trader   A business run by one person without being incorporated. Easy to start, but has unlimited liability

Stock days   The number of days' worth of purchases equal to the amount of stock you have on hand.

Working capital   Generally current assets less current liabilities. In Mergers and Acquisitions (M&A) this is taken as stock, trade debtors minus trade creditors, since cash is aggregated with debt.

BOOKS TO INSPIRE YOU

Andrews, Andy (2005) *The Traveller's Gift: Seven decisions that determine personal success*, Hodder Mobius

Blanchard, Ken and Sheldon Bowles (2007) *Gung Ho: Turn on the people in any organization* Financial Times/ Prentice Hall

Caan, James (2009) *The Real Deal: My story from Brick Lane to Dragon's Den*, Virgin Books

Denny, Richard (2009) *Selling to Win 3rd edn*, Kogan Page

Fisher, Roger and William Ury (2003) *Getting to Yes: Negotiating an agreement without giving in*, Random House Business

Frankl, Viktor (2011) *Man's Search For Meaning: The classic tribute to hope from the Holocaust* (with new material), Rider

Holmes, Dame Kelly (2006) *Black, White and Gold: My autobiography*, Virgin Books

Millman, Dan (2000) *The Way of the Peaceful Warrior: A book that changes lives*, H J Kramer

Robbins, Anthony (2001) *Awaken the Giant Within: How to take immediate control of your mental, physical, emotional and financial life*, Pocket Books

Simpson, Joe (1998) *Touching the Void*, Vintage

Tracy, Brian (2010) *No Excuses: The power of self discipline*, Vanguard Press

FEATURED BUSINESS OWNERS

James Caan
James Caan Is the founder and CEO of Hamilton Bradshaw, based in London, and co-founder with Bev James of the Entrepreneurs' Business Academy. He is well known as a former investment 'dragon' on the highly popular BBC TV show *Dragons' Den* and is currently working alongside the UK Government as a member of the Entrepreneurs' Forum to help and advise the Business Secretary on new business policies.
www.james-caan.com

Jamie Constable
Jamie is the founder of RCapital with business partner Peter Ward. He provides turnaround funding and management expertise to companies in financial distress. To date, RCapital has purchased twenty-four companies in deals ranging from £1 million to £20 million, including the iconic roadside Little Chef chain featured on Channel 4's *Big Chef Takes On Little Chef,* featuring Heston Blumenthal.

Roja Dove
Roja Dove, the perfumer, is founder of The Roja Dove Haute Parfumerie at Urban Retreat, Harrods, London. He is author of The Essence of Perfume (Black Dog Publishing) and creator of Roja Parfums. www.rojadove.com

Matt Dyer

Matt Dyer is the founder, CEO and sole shareholder of ITC Compliance Ltd, the UK's largest independent Financial Services Authority compliance network. www.itccompliance.co.uk.

Gill Fielding

Gill Fielding is an international motivational speaker, business-woman, presenter and author. Despite being born into humble beginnings in the East End of London, she is now a self-made multimillionaire who enjoys sharing her knowledge on wealth creation, financial education and investing skills to help others succeed. She owns or co-owns a variety of businesses today, including The Wealth Company, and is a published author. Gill was featured on *The Secret Millionaire* (Channel 4) and was a business expert on *The Apprentice – You're Fired* (BBC 2).

Penny Power

In 1998 Penny founded www.ecademy.com, the UK's first social network for business, with her husband, Thomas. Ecademy is now a global operation with members in more than two hundred countries.

Paul Ragan

Paul Ragan founded Motaquote, the insurance brokerage company based in Cardiff, at the age of 23 after leaving school with few qualifications. Motaquote grew into a multimillion-pound business and became the leading UK independent insurance broker in Wales. When the business was sold in 2008, Paul became one of Wales' youngest multimillionaires. In addition to managing his own investment fund, he is founder of the Collateral Thinking consultancy.

Mark Rhodes

Mark Rhodes is a self made millionaire entrepreneur, business mentor and success coach. He is in demand internationally as a motivational speaker. www.rhodes2success.com

Peter Thomson

Peter became an entrepreneur in 1972 and has built three successful companies. He sold the third company for £4.2 million, after only five years of trading, which enabled him to retire at the age of 42

Emma Wimhurst

Emma Wimhurst is a much-sought-after motivational business speaker and business turnaround expert. She is a successful entrepreneur (having founded Diva Cosmetics), broadcaster and regular contributor to UK media. She is author of *BOOM! 7 Disciplines to CONTROL, GROW and ADD IMPACT to Your Business.*

INDEX